Praise for *I'll Take New Haven*

"Lary Bloom's *I'll Take New Haven* is to New Haven what James Heriot's *All Things Wise and Wonderful* is to the Yorkshire Dales and veterinary life post World War II. These are delightful, much-needed tales that will warm your heart and reaffirm your faith in humanity—and with an adorable scene-stealing puppy to boot."

—**Molly Gaudry**, author of *We Take Me Apart*

"For decades, Lary Bloom was one of the foremost chroniclers of Connecticut life, which too often meant Hartford life, or Connecticut River Valley life. But a few years ago he had the wisdom to move to New Haven, and we Elm City denizens had the good sense to welcome him. Now, as if to thank us, or pay down a debt, he has produced this beautiful, winning collection of essays about re-urbanizing oneself, and one's spouse, in life's third act. It's a terrific read by my terrific neighbor."

—**Mark Oppenheimer**, author of *Squirrel Hill: The Tree of Life Synagogue Shooting and the Soul of a Neighborhood*

"In a world where the sun burns cold and cyborg overlords rule the land, humanity prays for a hero. That hero is Lary Bloom, bringing warmth, whimsy and wisdom to life in New Haven and reminding his reader that every day contains a good story, if you see it and tell it right. I wish some of the cyborgs would read this book, especially YW-1183 who just doesn't get us."

—**Colin McEnroe**, WNPR host, columnist, author of *My Father's Footprints*

"Amble down the path of New Haven's city streets with Lary Bloom and you'll want to pack up and move to the Elm City with Bloom as your guide. The book is packed with tidbits of wisdom and is not just a great read but a wake-up call, inviting us into our own innate humanity."

—**Nancy Slonim Aronie**, author of *Writing From the Heart* and *Memoir as Medicine*, founder of the Chilmark Writing Workshop

"With his characteristic curiosity, humor, and insight, Lary Bloom's essays help us make sense of these challenging times, and to find compassion for those we disagree with—and ourselves."

–**Sarah Darer Littman**, author of *Deepfake, Anything But Okay, Backlash,* etc.

"Chronologically challenged columnists don't fade away; they simply get better. Lary Bloom's recent portfolio brings fresh eyes to New Haven's land- and people-scape. A recent immigrant from the provinces, he writes with wonder and affection about his brave new urban habitat."

–**David Holahan**, award-winning essayist

"In *I'll Take New Haven*, Bloom reminds us to listen, observe, engage and care as he unfolds tales from the streets of New Haven and his own layered life as a young widower, Vietnam veteran, IRIS family sponsor and new dog owner. This book feels like a private visit with the droll, sharp grandmaster of Connecticut's writing scene."

–**Mary Collins**, author of *At the Broken Places: A Mother and Trans Son Pick up the Pieces*

"I spent several hours with Lary Bloom's *haimishe* voice in my head and found it a very pleasurable experience. I was familiar with some of the essays that I read in the Independent but many of them were new to me. The effect of reading them this way, in a collection, lends the work a gravitas that sometimes gets lost in the blur of the daily news cycle. It reminded me of Alfred Kazin's *A Walker in the City*, that writer's midlife musings on his coming of age as a young man in Brooklyn. In *I'll Take New Haven* the *flaneur* is Lary Bloom, a writer musing on his coming-of-old-age in the city he adopted late in life. Bloom's love of his city, of his wife, and of his dog (not necessarily in that order) permeates every well-observed snapshot."

– **Donald Margulies**, Pulitzer-winning playwright of *Dinner with Friends, Time Stands Still, Brooklyn Boy, Sight Unseen,* etc.

"Lary Bloom has been a voice for sanity, humanity, and the appreciation of quiet beauty in Connecticut for a lifetime. How lucky New Haven is that he chose to train his eye and his craft on our society in his golden

years! Whether you live in New Haven, think about living in New Haven, or simply have an interest in how colorful, striving communities work, this collection of essays will open your eyes and your heart."
–Paul Bass, editor, *New Haven Independent*

"Woof."
–Lucca, resident Lagotto Romagnolo

ALSO BY LARY BLOOM

Sol LeWitt: A Life of Ideas

The Writer Within

Letters from Nuremberg (with Christopher J. Dodd)

The Ignorant Maestro (with Itay Talgam)

The Test of Our Times (with Tom Ridge)

Lary Bloom's Connecticut Notebook

Something Personal

When the Game Is on the Line (with Rick Horrow)

I'LL TAKE NEW HAVEN

Tales of Discovery and Rejuvenation

Lary Bloom

Antrim House
Bloomfield, Connecticut

Library of Congress Control Number: 2022910019

ISBN: 979-8-9855621-2-5

First Edition, 2022

Printed & bound by Ingram Content Group

Book design by Rennie McQuilkin

Cover design by Erica Udoff

Cover illustration: detail from 1905 postcard reading "Junction
Elm & Broadway, New Haven, Conn." (Reichner Bros., artist unknown)
with silhouettes of the author and Lucca

Author photograph by Suzanne Levine

Antrim House
860.519.1804
AntrimHouseBooks@gmail.com
www.AntrimHouseBooks.com
400 Seabury Dr., #5196, Bloomfield, CT 06002

To Susan and Joel Jacobson, and Roxanne and Kevin Coady,
who led us to this new adventure.

ACKNOWLEDGMENTS

Any book undertaking, as writers well know, requires the help of many others whose generosity of spirit and expertise make such an effort possible. In my case, I have had the benefit, since arriving in New Haven, of the guidance of a consummate editor, Paul Bass, founder of the New Haven Independent, who in an era when local journalism has declined has created for the Elm City a model for the nation. (Indeed, his epic effort, the roots of which extend to the late 1980s, is chronicled in *The Wired City*, by Dan Kennedy.) Most of the essays in this book appeared in a slightly different form on the Independent's website (www. newhavenindependent.com).

Rennie McQuilkin, the editor and publisher of this book and a former Poet Laureate of the state, has been a champion of Connecticut poets and writers over many decades, as both the founding director of The Sunken Garden Poetry Festival and publisher of Antrim House.

The graphic designer (and humorous philosopher) Erica Udoff created the wrap-around cover of this book. Nina Lentini and Karen Cantillon, excellent copy editors, helped polish the manuscript.

And, as has become so important to my work over many years, the poet Suzanne Levine, who also happens to be my wife, took on the work of being my initial editor, and offered her wisdom, as always, on how to choose the right word, and to make sense of things.

There are others, too, who have been involved. If I start naming everyone I can think of who had a hand in this, I fear I will leave someone out. Still, I thank you all.

TABLE OF CONTENTS

A man's work is nothing but this slow trek to rediscover, through the detours of art, those two or three great and simple images in whose presence his heart first opened.   –Albert Camus

I'LL TAKE NEW HAVEN

Tales of Discovery and Rejuvenation

A Brief Word About Longevity

I believe in free will. I have no choice.
–Isaac Bashevis Singer

When my wife Suzanne and I decided in 2015 to move from the tranquil countryside to urban chaos and culture, friends were surprised, and so were we.

We had vowed never to leave our barn house in the woods of Chester, home for three decades. That town has barely 4,000 residents, with a village center of old-world charm, small-shop commerce, and an air of affability. In a way, it is a mystical place, even willing to laugh at itself; its semi-official slogan: "Chester, CT: We Know Where It Is."

So news of our flight from this tiny Brigadoon astonished more than a few locals. *New Haven? Really? We love it for its theater and music and art and of course the pizza but what about high city taxes and gunshots in the night and . . .*

Most weren't even aware of another Elm City distinction: the selection in 2016 by Conde Nast Traveler as one of the ten unfriendliest cities in America. Hence, we presumed, should we slip on sidewalk ice, a distinct possibility considering our senior citizen status, a majority of witnesses would simply step over us.

Nevertheless, in our resolve to add ourselves to the city's climbing census count (134,023 in 2020) we were far from alone. Many people who've reached retirement age inhabit these old streets, drawn by satisfactions untallied by magazine list makers whose research favors police blotters, city budgets, and stereotyping over the more difficult task of assessing quality of life.

On these pages, I have taken the trouble, because I have no choice, of documenting the results of exurb-to-city adventure. Every time I have a religious experience, having nothing to do with theism but a kind of movement of soul, there's a tale to write.

The yarns that follow trace how I became content in this place of urban complexities, rewards, heartbreak, and delight. Some of it is borne out of the perils of aging. But these findings are relevant for younger people—just about everyone I meet these days—because they contain useful lessons drawn from decades of personal experience, observation, failure, and sources of exultation. In short, what matters in the true end, when life itself turns fragile.

In these days of ours, we may have no choice about free will, but we have options aplenty about almost everything else.

Sidewalkers

One early spring day while finishing a walk around the block, I came across a woman about my age with a cane, backpack and an expression that said, "Let's have a chat."

She nodded toward the pup on my leash, and, as most foot travelers, was eager to pet little Lucca, a fluffy Italian water dog.

While she did so, I resumed my hobby of digging for New Haven gold, defined here as a pedestrian's daily discovery and illumination. It's a habit. I meet a fellow walker, and the questions fall out of my mouth.

"Walk here often?" I said, though it sounded a bit like a pickup line.

"Yes," she said. "I love this neighborhood. You meet so many interesting people." However, she didn't specify whether I was one of them.

I said, "Tell me, what street do you live on?"

"Oh, I don't. I used to live here in the city, very near this spot, actually. But I've been in Wallingford for many years. I just like to come back here whenever I can to walk."

Well, dear reader, you may be relieved to know that I did not pry further, did not ask, "If you love it here, why did you leave it?"

The woman turned the conversation to a neighbor's yard. As almost all walkers in this vicinity, she had stopped to observe Orange Street's top tourist attraction, a house with no lawn.

"It's gorgeous," she told me. "I wish more people had the taste and guts to do this."

"Yes," I said, but didn't add that when the home owner next door, a retired Yale professor of archeology, first dug up her grass many years ago and planted nothing but flower beds, she heard complaints from local landscape purists.

"It's a bit of a neighborhood metaphor," I said. In New Haven, life as we expect it is often upended by, among darker things, in-your-face beauty and innovation and by people who have lived long enough to know that it's a fool's errand to please everyone else when you don't please yourself.

Soon, the woman was ready to continue her walk, and said, "Perhaps we'll meet again. I'll be back, that's for sure."

Ah, the sidewalks in our city, paths to illumination. On pleasant or subpar weather days, they are packed with humanity.

Sometimes Lucca and I sit on the front stoop and watch it all go by, and I try to explain to him the context of living in the section of the city called East Rock.

"Look, Mr. Muffin Head (one of the pup's nicknames), across the street to the left is where that congenial lawyer resides who drives the Mercedes convertible and a Harley. He defends accused drug dealers, robbers and murderers, as he says, 'bad people—but somebody has to do it.'

"And over there to the right is the empty storefront that a buyer would like to fill with a shop that sells ice cream and alcoholic beverages — well, city life, the juxtaposition of wholesomeness and bacchanalia. That spot, Lucca, was until recently a Syrian market, where we bought the hummus wraps you tried to snatch from our shopping bag. That's another name for you, isn't it, Master Pickpocket? We didn't know at the time how relevant Syria, and its civil war, would become to us.

"Well, puppy, don't look at me like that. Life is complicated. I'll explain more later. For now, understand the diversity of this place. Over there, directly across the street, are the Chinese immigrants who bought three houses on this block, refurbished them, repaved the driveways, and planted new grass and gardens as lures to grad students to rent because the neighborhood is sometimes called, indelicately, 'the Yale Ghetto.'

"Speaking of properties that have rental apartments, Louise, who always makes a fuss over you, Mr. Fur Ball, owns the three-family house to our left. She has lived there her whole life, like a lot of the Italian-Americans who settled this area. That spectacularly red Japanese maple tree in her backyard was planted in 1941, the year she was born.

"She rents the third floor to Emily, whom I mentioned to you, though you didn't seem to be paying attention, is one of the East Rock's many post docs—you can hardly walk down the sidewalk without bumping into one of them and knocking over her latte—but presumably Emily is the only PhD holder who wrote a dissertation on dragon flies. She assures me they are an important part of our eco system and, like so much else, endangered, as their wetland habitats disappear."

From our front stoop, Lucca often joins me as I infringe on the personal space of pedestrians. He is curious about everything. And the old journalist in me can never be satisfied. Who are these people? What can I learn from them? For without learning, we are essentially without a pulse.

When Lucca and I are not on the stoop, we are out there ourselves, two sidewalkers, unearthing things.

There is the matter of sidestepping book-reading pedestrians. New Haven is the only place in which I have lived where people on their daily strolls stick their heads into novels and non-fiction volumes. I wonder how they can do it without tripping on the uneven rose-colored pavement, much of which was installed a century ago. But books, the old-fashioned kind, bound and with purposeful aromas, their margins sometimes cluttered with notes, are part of the character of the neighborhood.

"Lucca, look," I say, knowing full well he will not make much of the miniature front-yard libraries that invite passersby to take books or leave them. These are constructed by generous neighbors who cultivate the joy of literature, from which Gigi

(Suzanne uses this name for interactions with grandchildren and dogs) and I have retrieved a variety of excellent volumes, and deposited ones we owned that we think will be of interest to others.

"Lucca, to tell you the truth, we have even put books we've written in these little libraries, not so much out of charity but out of ego curiosity. Blessedly, they were all taken by readers, but not as quickly as the work of, say, Danielle Steel or James Patterson."

In these treasured places, I found Amy Tan's *The Joy Luck Club*. I was introduced to the magnetic Jack Reacher novels by Lee Child, and Philip Roth's first book, *Letting Go* (1962). I came across a richly illustrated copy of Herman Melville's *Moby Dick* and a first edition of Toni Morrison's *Beloved*. William L. Shirer's *The Rise and Fall of the Third Reich* now has an honored perch on top of my toilet's water tank.

Lucca, we have discovered, is a book lover himself. In general, he prefers chewing paperbacks rather than hardcovers.

The pup and I have watched little readers walk hand in hand with parents on their way to the Worthington Hooker Elementary School on the corner of Canner and Livingston. They have chalked on the steps of the school, "Teachers Are Amazing. Thank you!"

True, interactions with children sometimes bring surprises, and illustrate the unusual population mix.

One morning, I saw a small boy walking with his mother. The boy was pushing the stroller in which, I presumed, he had been sitting. Little kids love to do that. I asked him about it. But he did not answer. I thought, well, he's probably taught not to speak to strangers.

Then his mother said, "Please understand. We just moved here, and so far he only speaks Portuguese. He's too shy to try his English."

As we learned, the boy was one of a legion of pint-sized immigrants, or sons and daughters of immigrants, who inhabit

East Rock. When we moved into the house, one of the former owners told us that Halloween was their favorite holiday: "The United Nations will come to the door."

We had been skeptical, and purchased, foolishly, only about 500 pieces of candy for our first Trick or Treat night. But hordes of Ninjas, princesses, Batmen, ballet dancers, skeletons and the like—many who were celebrating their first Halloween—descended, too many for our modest stock of goods. One child, perhaps four years old, had to be advised by parents in what seemed to be an Eastern European language not to enter the house, sit down at the piano and plunk out a tune.

On non-Halloween evenings, my own walks may bring me past outdoor tables of coffee shops and restaurants, where I can jaw with little ones who otherwise would enjoy an uninterrupted experience, but also where I can learn something from them.

At the Atticus Market, I met three-year-old Simmy. Her age was a statistic reported to me by her father, while sitting next to her at a picnic table. Simmy, however, was having none of the math calculations. "Actually," she said, munching on a croissant, "I'm three and three quarters."

And then she went on to advise me how to say that in Spanish, as she says she is studying that in nursery school. She also said she had lived in Brooklyn as well as New Haven, and has liked both places. Then she volunteered to give Lucca a treat from the bag hanging around my neck. I gave her a piece of kibble, and she put it in her right palm. This made me slightly nervous, as Lucca, though very friendly, is not always predictable. But he licked her palm and deftly lifted the piece of kibble. Simmy said, "Oh, he's so gentle."

She was obviously a bright child and also one whose physical features—she had blond waves and rosy cheeks—made me think later on about my daughter Amy, who was exactly Simmy's age when I took her to a park, put her on a swing, and explained to her that all living things must die. "Look at the flowers over there," I said pointing. "They bloom and are beautiful but they are not here forever." And then I broke the news that her mother had died in the hospital, though didn't get into the particulars of a brain aneurysm.

Since that time, I have wondered what was going on in that three and three-quarter year old head of hers at the time. I know very well what she said to me when I asked her, "Do you understand about death?" Her response: "Yes, I do, Daddy. All living things die. But when is Mommy coming home?"

My time with Simmy gave me some indication. That age is a significant one, as I learned eventually through work with the psychologist who taught me many things over several years of therapy. It is just at the point where the bonding between mother and child is complete, when trust is firmed up, when loss is understood but not grasped. Just at the point in a young life when the surviving parent can respond in an enlightened way or in a way that further complicates the child's life. When I think of what came afterwards, and the little that I knew, and the finite energy I devoted to keeping Amy on the road to recovery, I shudder. "I did the best I could," that old canard, rings hollow to me, and to Amy as well. But that story, and its conclusion, is part of the reason for my present level of contentment.

That's the thing about a good walk. It gets you out of the house and into the imagination. I had a mentor during my years in Miami, a famous writer so accomplished that in 1979 he was awarded the Nobel Prize in Literature. Every morning, Isaac Bashevis Singer walked the streets of his neighborhood, and on these journeys his mind took off in all directions. It was on his walks there and in other places where he lived (New York City and various places in Switzerland after emigrating from Poland in 1935), where he discovered, among many others, the complex characters named Yentl, and Gimpel the Fool, and the broken and uncivil Holocaust survivors in the novel, *Shadows on the Hudson*. He told me that the hour on the sidewalks was his connection to both life as he knew it and life as he interpreted it. He died in 1991, but I think of him on these walks, not only because it influences my own approach to work, but because I see things that spark the imagination. Even relatively frivolous things, though eating is not a frivolous enterprise.

A walk on New Haven's State Street in the evening might bring you to the sidewalk tables spilling out of The Tavern. There, you may see orders of a favorite appetizer, grilled octopus, which may intrigue you, or, in the case of a certain unnamed person in my household, gross you out. (But, if so, how can oysters be so necessary to her?)

These days, I seldom return from a vigorous walk without the warmth of some human interaction, and thinking I've learned something, either about someone, or about the nature of things, or about a hard-headed but loveable dog, or about something I'd seen a dozen times but never really stopped to notice.

I recognize that I may be labeled as one of those creepy old folks who roam the neighborhood, mischief on my mind. But, as we age, we assign more value to the lives of others and want to know how they navigated through the obstacles that appear in every life.

At funerals and memorial services, I learn fascinating things I didn't know even about dear friends while they were sitting at our dinner table. I want to know about people now, before they perish, and before I retire my curiosity, which I hope never happens.

We are not, by nature, listeners. We talk over each other. It infuriates me when at a dinner party guests interrupt and refuse to let the person holding forth finish the sentence. I admit I have sometimes done this myself. But I am always wary.

Writers notice everything: the cigar stubbed out on the street, the color of the lipstick left on the martini glass, the body language that may betray the spoken word. And sometimes, it takes a while to understand the truth.

Such as the sign on a neighbor's yard. "Flying Lessons: By Appointment Only." For months, I thought it might be serious, until I finally noticed the broom handle.

Free Lunch with Mahalia and the Duke

Back when Suzanne and I remained in residential limbo. we had rented an apartment in East Rock, just to try out urban life, an expensive experiment as we were still paying our mortgage for the Chester house.

Our thought, then, was to spend weekdays in the city and retreat to our real home on weekends. But as time went on, we abandoned the plan. There was simply too much to attract us in our new city.

New Haven defies certain statutes of Connecticut ("The Land of Steady Habits") that appear to prohibit acts of outrageous spontaneity. Hence, it's possible in this city to make a new plan for the day at any moment. The Yale calendar is a prominent source that inspires this untoward behavior. In non-pandemic times, the public can sign up for spontaneous erudition and delight, and damn the legal consequences.

So I knew I would have a lot of company when I went out the front door, turned right, walked fifty yards to the bus stop and awaited the Orange Line of the free Yale shuttle, which arrives every fifteen minutes or so in the morning and evening hours.

There was no need to pretend I was a professor emeritus or a student or alumnus. No requirement to dangle a lanyard with a big blue Y from my neck. No requirement to sing the chorus from Cole Porter's 1912 fight song, "Bulldog! Bulldog! Bow Wow Wow," or recite a secret code of Skull & Bones. We are all invited. We have all the qualifications necessary; we are residents of a progressive city that, daily, offers discovery and, on the shuttle, gratis transportation.

By then, before the scheduled appearance on campus of Stanley Crouch, the jazz critic and author and proponent of controversial notions, I already had been a veteran of such outings.

The Yale campus is where I met Mia Farrow in the days she tried to put her former squeeze Woody Allen in a vice, but, more significantly, awaken America to the hopelessness in Darfur. I heard Maya Lin, one of my personal heroes for her sculpture in the nation's capital about my ludicrous war, as she introduced us to her ambitious new landscape designs.

Roz Chast proved as witty a speaker as in her New Yorker cartoons. She presented her creative process for *Can't We Talk About Something More Pleasant*?, a book on her parents' denial of impending infirmity and the subject of mortality. The scribe Dominick Dunne and his former editor at Vanity Fair, Tina Brown, dished the dirt about Princess Diana. An expert on Dutch painting offered six lectures on the works of Vermeer, Rembrandt, Hals, and other luminaries of the period, followed by a champagne reception. Presentations about race relations throughout America's tortuous history on that score drew standing-room-only crowds. Screenings of new Italian films each April were augmented by the presence of their directors. All for free.

The stop at which I alighted from the Yale shuttle on this day was the corner of Temple and Wall, and from there it was but a short walk to the Whitney Humanity Center. There, in a packed room on the second floor, Stanley Crouch sat in front of the fireplace with his cane in hand, as he held forth on the matter of just one song that I'd never heard but that brought me back in time and introduced me to a new level of spirituality.

The one-song examination may have seemed to some an unusual idea for a program. But in my own work as writer, editor and teacher I have stressed narrow focus and intimacy, and this event showed the power of that approach.

For sixty minutes, students, professors and curious visitors from the community at large listened, responded, and contributed to meaningful silence. The centerpiece of it was one plea from Duke Ellington and his collaborators titled "Come Sunday," performed in a 1958 recording by Mahalia Jackson, the Queen of Gospel.

I was drawn to the session for many reasons. Some of them stemmed from memory. Even as a young fellow, I played Ellington's more popular melodies on the piano. "Mood Indigo" was a tune that resonated though I was not of the society from which it was inspired, and did not, at the age of fifteen, fully appreciate its power. "In My Solitude," the same. I was still years away from discovering the depths of clinical depression, and the paradoxes of parenthood or darkness of widowerhood (twice), or how great artists can express and interpret them in a deeper manner than psychologists.

As Crouch pointed out in his remarks, Ellington had managed through his elegance and talent to enhance an idea born in New Orleans by creating a whole new form of sophistication that transcended musical and racial boundaries.

As Crouch often pointed out in reviewing the history of jazz, Ellington wrote the blues even if his blues didn't fit within the classic twelve-bar format, because "sooner or later," Crouch said, "everyone gets them."

I thought back to that privileged moment in 1962 when, as a college freshman in Ohio, I saw and heard the Duke perform them. I did it because some instinct beyond the need to go to classes drew me to everything that came to campus — the visiting orchestras, ballet companies, poets, satirists, theatrical productions, political lectures, etc., and because as an amateur musician myself, I knew Ellington's work, or some of it.

I invited another freshman, a young woman. It was a first date. I had a lot of those. And I didn't know much about her, except that she was pretty and very quiet. She was dressed in a white silk blouse and a paisley skirt. I didn't think of it then, but later on it occurred to me she was, in effect, my "Satin Doll," the title of what may be the Duke's most popular song (written, like many, with

Billy Strayhorn), as she was both stunning and mum. (Though the song says the real Satin Doll speaks Latin.)

I paid little attention to her for long stretches; instead, transfixed by the orchestra leader, his smart checked black-and-white suit, the deep pockets of skin under his eyes, the long fingers that he slapped the keys with, and then his nods to cue his players for "Take the A Train" and "Sophisticated Lady," and "It Don't Mean a Thing if It Ain't Got That Swing."

During the ten-minute intermission, the musicians stood near the stage, some smoking, while drummer Sam Woodyard performed a solo, with a powerful crescendo, through the break. Then, one by one, the musicians went to their seats and started to join in. And in the second half there it was, deep into the night, "Mood Indigo," and by then I think my Satin Doll, who must have seen the tears in my eyes, had given up entirely on the idea of a second date. (That is a presumption, of course. She may have thought, instead, "Thank God there won't be a second date.")

I didn't actually feel mood indigo until years later. But when I did — on the occasion of the death of my first wife, mother of our only child, at the age of twenty-seven— this dark tune had become my theme song, and would stay my song until the pharmaceutical industry could train my fingers and heart to play something again in a major key.

Even though I had plunked my way into Dukeland, I didn't yet know the miracle of "Come Sunday," not until Stanley Crouch, rocking slowly in his seat and occasionally lifting his cane as if it was a conductor's baton, asked us in attendance to pause from our frayed and busy lives to stay awhile, to close our eyes, to really hear genius at work. He said that the blues, though often reflective of pain, could also uplift, and could reach places in the heart that may otherwise be remote.

Mahalia, he said, would show this.

The contralto, whom Harry Belafonte said at the time was

"the most powerful Black woman in America," sells every syllable in a song written long ago but speaks to elements of faith and the fight for freedom today. In part:

> *He'll give peace and comfort*
> *To every troubled mind*
> *Come Sunday, oh come Sunday*

But in these days of high technology, short attention spans, and the news that sanctuary is more in demand than ever, when the gains in understanding and mutual respect we have made in our country are in jeopardy, you should hear for yourself what Stanley Crouch wanted the dozens of us assembled to listen to that spiritual noontime several years ago, with no less than the Duke as accompanist to Ms. Jackson.

In 2020, when Ruth Bader Ginsburg died just two days after Crouch, an obituary recalled that whenever the associate Supreme Court justice felt angry, she sat down at the piano and practiced. The keys, black and white together, gave her comfort.

In the end, though Stanley Crouch was known, perhaps, more for his feistiness and activism than for his reverence, those of us who took advantage of that program (with a free buffet lunch, tuna and turkey and vegetable wraps and pastries, included) will recall an everlasting introduction to the intersection of melancholy and hope.

The Talking Hat

More than a half century ago, I wore a uniform of a different hue. The jungle fatigues and cap were manufactured in only one color, olive drab, which the military still refers to, drably, as Color 107. Unofficially, it was the shade of derision during and after America's most divisive foreign war.

These days, the uniform remnant I wear on the streets of New Haven hasn't a touch of old 107. On this cap of many colors, the yellow wording pops. Various versions of red, white, black, yellow and green recreate medals awarded to everyone who waded ashore, as I did in 1966, or landed in big silver birds at the airports of Da Nang, Cam Ranh Bay or Saigon, including those 58,209 Americans killed and the more than 2,500 gone missing before their Vietnam tours were at an end. The overall effect of the new uniform, then, is one that shouts.

No pussyfooting here. No, "Excuse me, but please forgive my participation in that tragic mess." For the modest cost of about $20, it announces "Vietnam Veteran" not once but four times, even on the back, should fellow pedestrians, lagging behind, miss the point.

And here in New Haven the change in response is hard to miss. As I walk the streets, sometimes without being consciously aware I'm wearing the cap, I am stopped by strangers. In a city whose residents are by and large opposed to war, the cap begins respectful conversation.

"Thank you," strangers say. To which I respond, "Thank you," because "You're welcome" seems inapt.

Some of these people tell me stories. Others reflect on that miserable time, and the waste of that war. Others tell me that nothing has changed, that ignorance and bigotry are still rampant. They despise the chicken hawks in the nation's capital.

Veterans of various wars tell me of their personal struggles, then and now. A man pushing a manual lawn mower in front of a house in East Rock, part of a landscape crew, tells me of his experience in Iraq. A woman in Edgewood Park, a former Marine, offers details of her tour in Kirkuk as her fiancé rests his head on a picnic table, apparently the victim of a drug hangover. A man walking with crutches and wearing a similar hat salutes and I return the sign of respect. A woman in the Amity wine store talks of her brother, who died from the effects of Agent Orange; her eyes well up as she says she doesn't know exactly where he was stationed, only that he was "out there." A middle-aged woman opens a shop door for me and says, "Veterans always go first."

A man in a city crosswalk is not as demonstrative but when he sees my cap he smiles wryly, as if we are old conspirators. A young woman on a bike thanks me as she passes by and I am startled, as young people usually don't respond to the hat. The middle-aged clerk, however, at a TYCO store on Elm Street gives me an 80-cent discount on a $5 copying bill, and when I thank him, he thanks me. Two young and strapping soldiers waiting for their baggage at the airport insist on helping me with mine, saying, "You've served our country, and this is the least we can do."

Stray comments occur in other places, too. A tobacco store owner in Lucca, Italy, tells me his dream is to visit Maya Lin's Vietnam memorial in Washington, D.C. A shoreline vet I have seen dozens of times and who wears his own Vietnam hat as if it's a permanent part of his body tells me, "I don't want to talk about the war." So even those who don't talk do talk, in some way.

Silence, of course, makes for empty narratives, and robs us of understanding. This was the case in all wars, but particularly ours. For how does one explain the very idea, as seen from today's perspective, of sending young men and many young women to do something that came to be seen as absurd and tragic on a scale that can never be measured in body counts?

My talking hat, then, remains both a symbol and a prompt. It has come to represent the very opposite of what was pervasive during the era of my return from war, when spit symbolized the national response to returning vets.

So my hat and I have become inseparable, a fact that sometimes irks my wife, a haberdasher's daughter, who is of the opinion that a night at the opera or Yale Rep requires a more appropriate lid.

And yet, with all this positive news, I wish I didn't have to include a couple of responses that made my sometimes thin skin crawl. The first was from a man about my age who, over drinks at a Yale event, wanted to know if I was in combat. I replied that in a great sense everyone who served in Vietnam was in combat, as almost all of us found ourselves in jeopardy. (My own experience, spent mostly in supply, included being ambushed and shot at, the bullet ripping through the jeep's canvas, six inches from the top of my head.)

He objected, saying only those in the Infantry and Artillery corps were in combat. I asked him where he served. He said he didn't. He took an educational exemption from the draft. "Ah," I replied. "I'd be careful if I were you about lecturing those of us who put our bodies on the line." And then walked away. (Afterwards, I was proud of myself for not punching him in the nose.)

I walked away from another incident with less satisfaction. It was the response of a worker in the New Haven tax office who proved at least 70 percent unhelpful and unenthusiastic in my effort to register for a tiny tax credit given to vets. She asked me if I wanted to apply it to property tax, car tax, or some other tax I can't recall. I asked for more information. She said, "That's not my job. Just tell me what you want to apply it to."

As a result, I made a choice under duress. And duress was the element of war that I hoped to leave behind a half century ago.

Still, these conversations remain but a small part of a more empathetic public response. It's true that an astonishing thirty-two years passed between my return from war and the first "Thank you for your service," an expression that in 1999 made me burst out in tears. But since then, members of the public have more than made up for the initial "homecoming." So on every Veteran's Day, and the days between, I salute you all.

I Gotta Have Heart

It began with a blackout and collapse. Yet that chilling event may have saved my life.

What follows here, a tale of bodily intimacies, is meant as a guide for the reader and a revelation that some medical miracles have lately become routine.

The story began on a late summer day in 2018. It had been brutally hot and humid. I walked to a market on Orange Street, dragging myself home, lugging cartons of 2 percent and almond milk.

"Take a bath," suggested Suzanne. "It'll help."

And so I did. I remember how calming it felt in the tub. What I didn't remember to do at the time was to keep the bathroom door open a crack, so that the air could circulate.

I stood up after a twenty-minute soaking to grab for the towel. A little while later, I woke up in the prone position.

For a moment, I felt a measure of comfort, welcoming the coolness of the bathroom tiles, but then thought, "Well, this isn't right."

A negotiation ensued. Suzanne was eager to call 911. I assured her I was okay, and just needed rest. She extracted a promise from me to call our primary care physician first thing in the morning.

The next day I earned an immediate appointment. Sue offered to drive me; I insisted she stay home. It was a twenty-five-minute trip from New Haven to Westbrook, and I was sure I could manage it. This bullheadedness is evidence that sanity is a casualty in a health crisis.

The journey, however, was without incident. But my normally amusing primary care physician, who always chats about the worthiness of New Haven restaurants and who reported after a recent yearly exam, "You are fermenting nicely," refused to crack a smile.

"You mean you drove here yourself?" he said. "Are you nuts?"

He didn't wait for an answer. Instead, he called for an ambulance to take me to Yale New Haven Hospital's emergency room in Guilford.

What does one think of during his first ride ever with EMTs? Is it too cold in here? What are all these machines? How will my wife get the car in Westbrook? Is this my day of reckoning? Are my underpants clean?

The Guilford experience was a blur. Within a few minutes I was back in a moving clinic and on the hospital's main campus in New Haven.

"Cardiac unit," I heard, as they wheeled me into a room.

"Cardiac unit?" Nobody in my family had ever been wheeled into such a place. My ancestors were burdened by cancer, not heart troubles.

Soon an attending physician indicated the issue at hand was unrelated. "You may have suffered from dehydration. However," the specialist said, "we need to do tests just to be sure." These, I learned, included an echocardiogram. It revealed, alas, that the period of "fermenting nicely" had ended.

I had developed a condition called aortic stenosis. Specifically, my primary heart valve was no longer opening properly. Hence, my blood wasn't reliably reaching its destinations, though at that point the condition was adjudged "mild to moderate."

Three summers later, though, after my collapse, test showed that "mild to moderate" had progressed to "severe," just one stop from "critical."

The following week I met the surgeon in charge of my case. He introduced himself as "Mike."

"Gee," I thought. "I don't need a Mike. I need a cardiac

wizard." I knew what Dr. Michael Cleman was doing, putting me at ease. In a way, I was already there.

Rather than panic, I felt blessed. At the age of 77, I was way ahead of the game. Living in an agreeable neighborhood in New Haven with the woman I love. Drawing strength from our combined families, and the achievements of our combined four children and eight grandchildren. Compiling a "permanent record" largely without prominent scandal or crushing failure. I had done things I never thought possible, including learning to speak Italian well enough to avoid being arrested for impersonating a bilingual traveler, pursuing my love of theater by writing plays and the lyrics for a musical, turning out enough books to lose track of how many, and teaching at Yale.

Even the idea that Suzanne and I now had a third member of the immediate family, little Lucca, our Italian pooch, provided comfort.

More than that, I was the beneficiary of contemporary medical developments. I didn't need open heart surgery to replace the valve. I could take advantage of the much less invasive procedure, through arteries in the groin, a technique known as TAVR (transcatheter aortic valve replacement), a groundbreaking method less than twenty years old but so common at 20 York Street that in the last two decades thousands of men and women have experienced it.

When I met with one of the surgeons on the cardiac team, she explained all this, as well as the possible upside. "You will likely have more energy afterwards," she said.

She also reported that the new valve would be crafted from tissue from a pig or a cow, and asked, "Do you have a preference?"

I said, "My preference is to delegate such delicate decisions to those with expertise. However, if you choose the pig option, please don't tell my rabbi."

Such medical authorities explain the risks involved in the surgery — including stroke and worse. As websites say, in effect, "You may experience death." That, of course, would be an unfortunate experience. I waved them aside. The percentages of failed procedures are minimal. Besides, this was not a case of elective surgery.

Preliminary tests were required: a CT scan, a stress test (which succeeded in giving me considerable stress, as my blood pressure yo-yoed), and an angiogram, in which I was introduced to the idea of slit arteries.

And then the big day. July 20, 2021, at 7 a.m.

Wheeled into the OR, I saw a team of at least six assembled, along with so much medical equipment that I gasped, "All this just for me?"

The last thing I remember was when the anesthetic, Propofol, sent me off into Lovely Land.

When I awoke in post-op, my kind nurse, Dee, who had just started her twelve-hour shift, revealed that all went well. Her kindness and expertise were needed for many hours; her workday was almost over before the hospital found a free room in the cardiac ward.

During that time, and later, a parade passed through, intent on examining the incisions.

"Mind if I check your groin?" doctors asked one after another.

In my lingering haze, I heard the same question about groin-checking from other physicians as well as practical nurses, registered nurses, assistants to nurses, technicians, custodians, cooks, flower shop customers, accountants, and the New Haven Symphony.

I'm sure you are asking yourself right now: "Okay, so the important part of the two-day, one-night vacation went well, but how was the food?"

My answer is: Yale New Haven has excellent doctors and nurses who know what they're doing. The kitchen? I don't rate it among the top twenty in our fair city.

For lunch I ordered a grilled cheese, vegetable soup and a fresh fruit cup. This arrived forty-five minutes later in the form of Birkenstock-dry chicken breasts and salt-free chicken soup.

"I've never seen that happen before," testified Dee. Hours later, taking pity on me, she smuggled in a warm blueberry muffin.

That night, finally ensconced in room 16 on the cardiac floor, I couldn't sleep, read, or even watch TV. Naps came in fifteen-minute increments.

In a period of consciousness, I overheard my new nurse talking in the hallway to a colleague. "Every morning when I get home, she greets me with, 'Good morning,' and 'I love you.'" Her colleague remarked, "That's amazing, considering how young she is."

When the nurse came into my room to carry out yet another groin check, I asked her about what I presumed was her precocious toddler. "No," she said. "It's not a child. It's my dog who says that."

I thought: This must be the anesthetic doing cartwheels in my brain. But I thought of little Lucca, who during his eight months of life with us to that point had not yet, even once, inquired, "Well, master, how do you feel today?"

The next afternoon, after an echocardiogram confirmed my new valve is living up to expectations, I was released. Exhausted but relieved. Lucky this time. I was the beneficiary of fate, irony, medical advancement, and a platoon of caring and skilled professionals.

Two weeks later I learned that my new valve is kosher, made from cow cells.

Suzanne and Lucca were comforting, though the latter has been lax at proper nursing care. Still, I am happy to see him barking at life as if it will last forever.

The Muslim Ban Hits Home

Let me start, as I must, with the election of Donald J. Trump as president in 2016. In our neighborhood, there was no diversity of opinion. There was disbelief and despair. The party that we had organized with our two upstairs neighbors to celebrate Hillary Clinton's victory — we had baked a cake and uncorked Veuve Clicquot, and Suzanne had placed photos of her mother and grandmothers in a prominent spot — devolved into a frightful hangover.

But my point here is diversity, not Trump lament, except as it applies to that question. From the very beginning of his candidacy, bigotry became official policy, and it manifested in cities such as ours that were sanctuaries for new legal refugees (and, yes, a population of illegals as well). First came the shouts of Mexican criminals, and then the Muslim ban, and then the clamping down on all immigrants from countries that don't hold the promise of, when they become citizens, voting Republican.

What could be done? Rail on Twitter or Facebook? Of course. But what then, after whistling into a hurricane? This is where the city comes in, because in the city there is always a movement against the tide, always a team of fighters, always a place to put energy that would otherwise be spent in wasteful ways.

This phenomenon helps distinguish city life from suburban life in that it lures residents into struggles for social justice. Most can't resist because in a diverse city like this they see beyond dreadful headlines to the humanity in their midst. Right across the street from us, a family of Syrian immigrants had established a stable business, a small market featuring Middle Eastern foods. When we came to order our hummus sandwiches or chicken shawarma, we could see in their faces and hear in our conversations the way the civil war back home had affected them.

I wrote to the organization called IRIS (Integrated Refugee and Immigration Service), three blocks from our house, and asked if I could become a "cultural companion" to new immigrants. A few evenings later, I was invited to a meeting of volunteers in which the need and the program were outlined. Hundreds of families, many from the Middle East as a result of the Syrian civil war, had arrived in New Haven, and IRIS's mission was to support their transition from the troubled world they knew into life in America. This would include housing subsidies, job searches, language classes, arrangements for medical tests, and other related aids. The idea for cultural companions was one of encouragement and engagement. The hope was that those chosen would be available once a week, for a period of no longer six months, to check in with the new refugees. When I explained the job to Suzanne, she was eager to join, and so the two of us committed to the task. What we didn't know at the time was that of all the combinations of immigrants and companions that IRIS arranged over the years, ours would be the most complex and challenging, and lasted not six months but several years, and would require of us and our refugee family every ounce of emotional strength, persistence and political action we could summon.

Our introduction to this came on an April day in 2017. IRIS had sent a representative and an interpreter who could translate from the Arabic, with us to a neighborhood in Westville, one of the city's finer locations where home values are high and crime rates are low, but which also has a variety of low-income housing units. It was in one of these, on Central Avenue, that we first met Haitham Dalati, then age 60, and his wife Shiyam Daghestani, 56.

We sat in the living room, furnished with donated items to IRIS. Shiyam made tea for all of us, and brought out homemade pastry. We could sense both her shyness and sadness. She smiled, but kept her comments to "Hello" and "Thank you," the words she knew in English. Haitham, on the other hand, had no difficulty expressing himself in our primary language, as he had learned it as a boy.

"We are so happy to meet you, Mr. Lary," Haitham said, then extended his hand to Suzanne. He had a shock of blond hair and wide blue eyes, defying the common picture of a new refugee from Syria. Shiyam, though, wore traditional Muslim garb, her hair wrapped in a hijab.

The IRIS official explained to Haitham, who translated for Shiyam, that Suzanne and I would help them adjust to their new land. We had no idea whether it was a wise fit in that no reference had been made to our own Jewish heritage. Among the things I didn't know at that point was that when Haitham was a child, living with his family in a community built around a British petroleum site, his father told him, "If you should see a Jew, he will kill you."

It had been decades since Haitham harbored any such fear. Others had replaced it. The ripping apart of the family's life in Syria, the loss of livelihoods, the terror of the civil war that began in 2011 and crimes on citizens committed by the country's leaders, the fleeing to Lebanon, where the language was familiar but where that society, too, was breaking down. And then the existential fear in the spring of 2017, when all was supposed to be well for the family, and the unthinkable happened.

In Washington, D.C., the new U.S. President had formulated and signed Executive Order 13769, titled "Protecting the Nation from Foreign Terrorist Entry in the United States." The title I would give it is "Fear Mongering Always Works for a Demagogue." It was intended as a total ban on Muslim integration. For almost all families on the verge of coming to the U.S., this became a deep disappointment. For Haitham and Shiyam, the timing of the administration had ripped their family apart.

All eight of them had applied to come to the U.S. from Lebanon through a United Nations refugee program, and all, after interviews, investigations and medical screenings, had been approved. So, in February 2017, they had tickets on two international flights out of Beirut. Haitham and Shiyam were booked on the first, and their daughter, Farah, son-in-law Wesam, and grandchildren Layla, Haitham, Lamese and little Abdul Salaam, the five-year-old whom everyone called Aboudi, were to follow a few days later. When Haitham and Shiyam were in the air, Trump struck. Only the patriarch and matriarch would enter the U.S. The rest were barred. And, along with that came the likely prospect that Haitham and Shiyam would never see their daughter or grandchildren again.

Aside from the inhumanity, this was also a singular circumstance. In almost all cases, it's the young people who come first and then, once settled, they invite the seniors. In this case, two grandparents, both of them with compromised physical health, particularly Shiyam, were left on their own, with only the institutional support of the local charity. And us.

One of the things that drove us to help was Judaism's tenet of *tikkun olam*, repair of the world. This very idea may seem pretentious and undoable, but our interpretation is that we have a duty to contribute in some way toward that goal. We were aware, of course, that in the Middle East the matter of the relationship between Muslims and Jews is much different than anywhere else, intensely affected by the history of the land, cycles of retribution, incessant warfare, suicide bombings, and oppression. The conversations about it are often characterized by extremist views, in part understandable because of the heavy personal prices so many on all sides of this have paid.

But heavy prices in the Middle East have been levied far beyond Israeli borders, and since 2011, in particular, the devastation suffered by the Syrian people has been immeasurable. We'd read about its civil war, of course. We'd seen the rubble as shown on the PBS NewsHour. But the war had not been brought home in human terms. So, in short, we knew very little.

I could sense in those first few minutes together with Haitham and Shiyam, they found it impossible and perhaps even distasteful to reveal in a first meeting the horrors of the Syrian reality, the destruction of all they held dear, the loss of livelihood and family and hope in a war that, for all of its length and statistical measures of catastrophe (nearly 4,000 dead, including 350 children), never summoned American outrage the way Russia's invasion of Ukraine would years later. Some of the reasons are obvious. And one of them is the abundance of racism and xenophobia that helped elect Trump in the first place.

CNN wasn't on the scene when the family lost their home in the bombings of the city of Homs. And the villa that served as their weekend escape northeast of the city went up in flames, the result of a missile attack, as they watched. They escaped death only because a warning had been issued minutes earlier by the villagers who were members of the rebellion against the authoritarian leader of the country, Bashar al-Assad.

The human cost of that, as well as the need to hide in the woods from Syrian troops as the family escaped to Lebanon, had been heavy, much too heavy for any light "cultural companions" to ease.

That was the matter, we learned, that would keep us tethered to the couple far longer than the prescribed six months, and would make it seem as if *tikkun olam* was just a fairytale.

Haitham told us on one of our visits that he and Shiyam had just spoken on Skype to the rest of the family, in Lebanon. He is a man who has a fine sense of humor, but also a fiercely protective side to him. He is not a crier. But he feels deeply, and at that moment, I could sense something was off, the direct result of the part of the Skype conversation that focused on the youngest child. Aboudi had said, "Grandfather, you promised you would take me to America. You lied to me. I will never trust you again."

Every Saturday, Suzanne and I drove from our East Rock neighborhood to Westville to meet our new friends. And every Saturday, we had to dissuade them from spending their limited funds on food for us. In most cases, we lost the argument.

Shiyam's lentil soup, for example, is of such flavor richness that our feeble attempts to recreate it at home have fallen far short. She made halal chicken and lamb dishes in the galley kitchen, showing Suzanne her steps. Though the two had no common language, they seemed to communicate well. Shiyam's eyes spoke eloquently, and often with sorrow. Whenever she asked Haitham to translate for her, and she talked of the family back home, tears dropped down her cheeks. In a way, though, as time went on, she drew comfort in the arms of Suzanne.

On occasion, we were able to persuade them to come with us for lunch. The first time we brought them to a middle eastern restaurant, Mamoun's, which is a New Haven institution.

It is a cozy place with Arabic songs on the sound system, and a menu full of traditional foods from the culture. The wait staff is bilingual and specializes in making customers feel at home.

As we waited for our food, Shiyam showed us new pictures of her daughter and grandchildren on her cellphone. They texted and spoke often to them when we were together. Their beautiful though saddened family became ours, too, as a result.

"Haitham," I said, "This is a place people hear about when they move to New Haven."

But if we thought it would impress them, we didn't yet know that Haitham possesses a quality that in the Jewish world is referred to as chutzpah.

While we ate our lunch, Haitham said, "Excuse me, Mr. Lary. I have to speak to the owner. This food is not authentic." (I kept telling him that he needn't refer to me as mister, but he persisted for the first year.) He then translated this for Shiyam who, motioning with her palms in the air, looked at us with an expression that said, "Well, that's my husband." She managed to say, in English, "No good." She was not referring to the lunch, but to what was about to happen.

But then we watched as Haitham and the manager of Mamoun's had what looked like a pleasant conversation. When Haitham returned to the table, he explained. "I told him the food doesn't have the right spices and is too salty to be authentic. He said he agrees, but he must cater to American tastes." This was far from the only time our outings led to unanticipated results.

The timing was right for a Yale Gallery exhibit on relics of ancient Syria. What better way would there be to reconnect Haitham and Shiyam to their homeland than by taking them to such an event. We could show them how, in this culture, at least in New Haven, there is an intense curiosity about the world, and groundbreaking civilizations. But we showed them nothing.

It was Haitham who guided us that day through the exhibition, stopping at each photograph, digitized map, antiquity and other suggestions of what this now ravaged country once looked like in all of its glory. He pointed out Homs, Shiyam's ancestral home, and made the exhibit come to life for us.

However, his intellectual savvy did not translate to the workplace. He needed a job, desperately, and it was not suitable to pursue anything in his profession as a lab technician. The effort to become certified in the United States would take years, and the family had an immediate need to meet mounting monthly expenses. As the IRIS subsidies subsided, Haitham became desperate for work.

I arranged for him to be interviewed at the local pharmacy, which needed drivers for its delivery service. At the time, Haitham didn't have a car, but managed to borrow one from a friend. He did well in the interview, and worked for two days, taking prescriptions from Orange Street to all parts of greater

New Haven, relying on his GPS. However, one of his fellow drivers, also an immigrant, told him that the pharmacy would cheat him, and pay much less than the service was worth. Haitham, who had by this time become wary of the ways of his new land, believed him. So he quit after two days.

Then, he received his pay in the mail. It was for $300, none of it taxable because it was in cash and under the table, for fourteen hours of work. He'd been bamboozled by a competitor who wanted to preserve his own income.

He applied for a job at a retirement community in nearby Hamden, and was given a place in the kitchen. As a foodie himself, he thought this might be a temporary solution, but in the second week, while lifting a tray of glasses, his right shoulder gave out, and he discovered, after a trip to the hospital, that recovery from torn muscles would take many months. So he had to resign from that as well.

In the meantime, their prospects to see their family again seemed just impossible dreams. Back in Lebanon, Farah and her family were making do. Her husband, Wesam, had a job in a bakery, and the children were all in school. But Farah could not stray far from home because of increasing violence by gangs against Syrian refugees.

Farah's family had no way to leave Lebanon as they no longer had passports. And even if their parents had the resources to travel, they couldn't ever return to Lebanon for a reunion because that government barred those refugees who left for America.

During one Skype session with the family, little Aboudi took aggressive action. "Grandfather," he said, "please give the telephone number of the White House. I think President Trump likes children. He would listen to me."

* * * * *

With each disappointment, Suzanne and I felt we had failed Haitham, Shiyam and the family. They always welcomed us with good cheer, and thanked us, but as we drove home Saturday after Saturday, we often felt as low as we ever had since our move. We were haunted by the idea we were failing our new friends.

We had reminded ourselves, however, of the power of momentum: to start somewhere, even at a very low point, and get forces moving in a positive direction. The first thing we did in hopes of a new beginning was to take Haitham and Shiyam to a place they would have never considered going.

Our idea: Bring Haitham and Shiyam to our synagogue in Chester, where we still belonged though it is forty minutes away, in large part because of its commitment to social action. Its members over its 100-year history had worked on behalf of civil rights, criminal justice reform, women's right to choose, and a host of other progressive issues.

I had discussed the idea with our rabbi, Marci Bellows, whose activism and quests for social justice were well known. She embraced the idea, and prepared for the evening. She wrote the congregation that we would have three special guests for Shabbat services. One, a staffer of IRIS, and the other two Muslim survivors of the Syrian civil war.

In a sense we were not alone in our efforts. Churches and synagogues around the state had found ways to aid in resettlement of war refugees by sponsoring families and otherwise supplying them with what they needed. But in many of those cases they were helping younger and healthier families. For the Dalatis, every new day without a breakthrough contributed to the mental and physical distress they wore on their faces and in their slowed movements.

And on that Shabbat night, the turnout was the largest we'd seen for some time. A reception and panel discussion was scheduled for after the service, but members didn't wait for that to offer their hugs to our friends.

At the point in the service when the rabbi usually delivers a sermon, she asked me to speak about Haitham and Shiyam. As I did, and told their story, I could sense the rapt attention from all parts of the sanctuary.

Here's part of what I said from the pulpit:

Haitham is often distraught, saying if he had to do it over again, knowing what he knows now, and having endured the pain that he and his family have endured, he would have stayed in Lebanon. He has also said, 'This is so horrible I don't know if America is good or bad for us.'

And yet we have also seen from our perspective something intimate to us, a glimpse into what the immigrants in our own families faced generations ago when they felt they were strangers in a strange land. Here, they have been able to find a community, a growing number of Syrian and Middle Eastern refugees who run businesses in West Haven, and a diverse community of immigrants from dozens of countries.

Haitham is a complicated man—confident in what he knows, and skeptical about what he has read or heard. As a child, he heard the talk among the adults that Palestinians are rightful owners of the land now called Israel. But he had read the Koran, which records the history of Israelites, and he asked himself: What is true, and what is false? That question, what is true and what is false, is one that any thinking person dwells on, especially one trying to adjust to a new land, to a new culture, to hang on to what he knows, and to learn what he doesn't.

He and I have found a certain kinship. During Ramadan, he confided that he isn't the most observant of Muslims in terms of the fasting demands of the holiday. I confided in him that I consider the twenty-four-hour fast at Yom Kippur to be a bit excessive and have lobbied here at the synagogue to reduce the fast to twenty-four minutes, but have not been successful in that pursuit.

When Haitham was a small child, perhaps only three years old, before most of his nine brothers and sisters were born, his mother gave him an orange, and she kept one for herself. He ate his hurriedly, while she was still working on hers.

He asked, 'May I have one piece of yours?" She began to cry, but not because she felt assaulted, ration-wise. She recognized something in her first born.

She gave him the whole orange. 'Here, Haitham, you eat. I don't like it.'

That wasn't really the case. She was just passing along nourishment from generation to generation, the very job we undertake today."

When I sat down, and the congregation began to sing one of its traditional Shabbat songs in Hebrew, Haitham put his right arm around my shoulder, and said, "Lary, we are so happy tonight."

Later on, we learned we were right about momentum. The chair of the social action committee, Andy Schatz, who had also served as president of the Connecticut branch of the American Civil Liberties Union, began to make inquiries even as Trump's Muslim travel ban stayed in place.

Suzanne, who once had served as a staff director in the Connecticut legislature, and who knew many people in state and national government, began to use her contacts, hoping for some way to get around the ban. I did the same, having worked in the past with high-profile public figures on their books.

Others were eager to help, but to that point, we had no word on whether their contacts were in any position to do so.

* * * * *

In November 2020, nearly four years since our first meeting Haitham and Shiyam, we prepped a small turkey in our New Haven kitchen, as the holiday in which we count our blessings became anxiety filled.

We awaited news from 506 miles away that would provide either another reason to rue a year of sorrow or show this dark world a light yet shines. And so, as the wine poured and cranberries cooked, our thoughts turned to Erie, Pennsylvania.

In the fall of 2019, quite unexpectedly, Haitham had called with the news that they were leaving New Haven and heading to the extreme northwest of the Keystone State. In that old industrial city, an emerging Syrian neighborhood was forming. Given that the city, like others in the Rust Belt, has suffered economically, it is much cheaper to live there as well.

Haitham found a job there, temporarily, working for an Israeli couple who owned a food market. Shiyam, meanwhile, made new friends.

During one phone conversation, I asked Haitham how Shiyam was doing with her English. He said, "Most people here can't speak it, so she doesn't get a chance. Compared to them, she is Shakespeare."

Then came this conversation, in November 2020, just as the election between Donald Trump and Joe Biden had been settled, though Trump was planning to challenge the results.

Haitham told us that Farah and her family were scheduled to be on a flight on Thanksgiving Eve to the United States. It turned out the federal government came through with visas after all.

But a part of us worried it would still never happen, that the Trump administration, amid a pandemic and still in power until Biden's inauguration, would find a way to continue blocking their entry.

Indeed, after Farah and the family arrived six hours before

their scheduled flight, they were held by Lebanese authorities. Some questioned why this family of refugees had such a right to travel to the United States. But almost at the last minute, they were released and had to run to the gate to make the scheduled flight from Beirut to Chicago.

Haitham texted us on Thanksgiving Day that they were in the air, and would stay in the Windy City one night, and then fly to Erie.

We heard nothing further, even as we stuffed that turkey down our gullets and ate too much of a delicious apple pie made by Atticus Market.

Then the next morning, Haitham sent us a video taken in the terminal at Erie International Airport. It is not a professional job, and at first there is no way to see the faces, but in the end, it all comes through. Suzanne and I watched in tears. The kind of tears meant for Thanksgiving, ones of gratefulness, and some inner light that refuses to go out.

We knew, too, that one day Farah and the rest would not just be figures on a screen but ones we would physically embrace.

Mill River Serenade

She was the woman who sat on the big rock on the bank of the river that runs through our neighborhood. She had a name, of course. But I never knew what it was, though she looked like a Martha to me. Perhaps it's because she mentioned that moniker once, and it stuck in my head. Our brief conversations mostly went nowhere. She seemed to think I was part of the Yale hierarchy, and asked if I knew this esteemed professor or that one. I simply said I didn't, and didn't bother revealing my modest status as a lecturer at old Bulldog U. Mostly, I'd say to her hello, such a nice day, how are you? Isn't it lovely here in the city yet also here at the Mill River?

She was not, I knew, the sort of nature lover who limited her astonishments to the renewing power of spring. "Martha," whom I judged to be in her mid-80s, was there in every weather, in every season, almost every day. At my front window, I'd marvel at her determined stride on the way to her destination, and think, my, she is showing us, dressed in her walking shoes, tights, dark sweater and flowing skirt, how to spend our remaining years.

But these days she no longer sits on the big rock next to the water, no longer smiles at my platitudes, and is nowhere to be seen.

My mind, of course, went into Covid-19 mode. In the most vulnerable age group, had she become a victim of that? Or something else? Or, is she still with us but for some reason unable to take that hike she took every day to the end of Orange Street and smack into a natural, almost untouched, setting?

Recently, on one of the first days of excellent spring, I returned to her perch, to seek clues. Clues of what, I wasn't sure. On that afternoon, I had company. Suzanne, our pooch, and our then 18-year-old grandson, Max.

Along the way, I snapped a photo of the rows of daffodils that stretch nearly fifty yards alongside the edge of East Rock Park. I have taken that same picture, from the same angle, every April.

In recent springs the beds of daffs take on deeper meaning. These flowers spring up no matter what happens around them, or what the city or the country or the world have gone through. Did "Martha" see the latest batch?

Before we arrived at her big rock, I looked up at the incline that reaches the top of the road, expecting to see what I had noticed a few days earlier. Someone had decided East Rock Park was a perfect place to dump two old pink couches.

The furniture appeared to have been tossed from a truck, and had taken down some of the greenery.

I had snapped a picture of the couches, thinking I might call the authorities. But now the furniture was gone, apparently whisked away by the park maintenance crew in their effort to keep a city asset pristine.

Down at the big rock, there was no sign of Martha. But the new puppy in our house has chosen this space as his own, as if he inherited it from her. He sat on her rock. And, as he suffered from the canine version of attention deficit disorder, he didn't stay long, waddling to the river's clear water, finding it delicious, and something that, up to his belly, felt just fine. He is, after all, an Italian water dog.

While we watched Lucca to be sure in this adventure he didn't get in over his head, Max saw a turtle out on a limb, sunning himself (or herself). This creature had previously hidden under his shell, blocking out any news of pandemics or political shenanigans or the outcome of the Super Bowl. The sun was what mattered. And he had it.

Meanwhile, music played. Not canned music. But the music of an outdoor soloist, somewhere in the vicinity, but I was not sure where it could be.

Fluid waves of tenor sax notes echoed throughout the valley, as if he had been hired to wake us up to what was happening. His sounds were not melodic, more like the runs of Sonny Rollins.

I mean, the man knew his instrument. I could tell he'd lived with it for years. But who was he, and where was he?

We crossed the footbridge over the river, with its new section built in 2020, with the names of those who built it etched into the wood, and we could still hear the music.

It had suddenly become familiar, specifically, the old ragtime tune, "The Entertainer," by Scott Joplin, something I've played on the piano since "The Sting" (with Robert Redford and Paul Newman as grifters) was released in 1973.

When I heard it, I wanted to skip along, but it was my grandson, whose bones are sturdy, who moved, running with the puppy across the terrain.

Fortunately for Suzanne and me, the pace returned to something a turtle could manage.

Many runners passed us, and quite a few of them wore dark blue masks with a white Y on the bottom left. These sons and daughters of Eli were on a mission, seemingly delighted to do this huffing and puffing in a space where skunk cabbage and willow trees showed their new spring green.

Perpendicular to Livingston Street, we cut into the open space where children gather and play. Suzanne and Max and the puppy were eager to get back home, but I did a detour.

Suzanne had spotted the man who was making the music for all of us. He was sitting on a park bench, facing the water below. "I have to talk to him," I said.

She replied, "Of course you do." She's used to my, as she calls it, "giving the third degree" to humans within range and she rolls her eyes skyward.

I wandered over slowly, not wanting to stop his playing. Eventually I took a seat near him. And then he stopped, and we talked.

I complimented him on his impromptu performance. I didn't have to pay Blue Note prices to hear his wonderful sounds. Indeed, he was a musician who had been around the block a thousand times, but only occasionally around New Haven blocks.

Except for a period in his life when he lived in the Elm City, Lee Mixashawn Rozie has always resided in his native Hartford. He knew all the great musicians of that city, including Jackie McLean, one of the world's most respected alto sax players.

More than that, using his history and ethnomusicology degree from Trinity College, he created "wave art," which is mostly what we were hearing.

Sitting on his bench he looked up at the 366-foot tall basalt deposit that gives East Rock its name. "Even that is part of a wave," he said, referring to impermanence of what seems like permanence.

He was in our town, he said, because the man who repaired his instrument is here. So, because it needed repair, we had all become the beneficiaries.

That's the nature of nature, isn't it? Something negative happens. Some gift comes out of it.

But the music didn't end when I pulled myself away from his bench. I saw an array of young people underneath the pavilion near the edge of the park. They were singing, and dancing, and the words were none I'd ever heard before.

These kids, socially distanced, were really into it, being led by their director, who was teaching them new steps and how to project the songs that emerged.

I excused myself and asked one of the young participants what was going on. She told me this was a rehearsal of the United Girls' Choir, featuring performers from age 5 to 17, which I had never heard before.

They looked so delighted to do this music, which, I was told, comes from South Africa, with origins mostly in Soweto, which before the end of apartheid, had been the site of so much oppression and terror.

At that point I thought of Martha and the big rock that was once hers. She was, apparently, gone, but not her nature.

Thornton Wilder, the iconic playwright and novelist who built a house Hamden in 1929 with proceeds from his book, *The Bridge of San Luis Rey* (he referred to it as "the house that a bridge built."), wrote a much lesser known drama than *Our Town*, the one-act *The Long Christmas Dinner*, in which the dining room table is the primary character in the action, which covers ninety years in an old house.

A family of many members gathers for the holiday celebration, and two or three of the characters are replaced by new ones in each scene. Eventually, every original character is gone, but life and legacy go on.

The nature of the occasion stays the same. The generations that celebrate it become a casualty of nature.

And yet something endures. An idea. A new face. A new song.

Something, Perhaps, About "The Game"

If you missed the big shindig at the Yale Bowl in November 2021, an afternoon of near perfect football weather, you avoided a crowd of about 40,000 there to see the Crimson and Sons of Eli take the field for the 137th time. So did we, almost.

I mistakenly thought it would be possible, given that we had paid two months in advance for reserved seats and parking, to arrive near kickoff, no problem. It soon seemed to us, however, that every car and SUV lately manufactured in Detroit, Sweden, Italy, Germany, Japan, Korea and Tennessee were ahead of us on the way to the west side of New Haven, all of them trying to turn left at one traffic light.

Though the first quarter had slipped by already, we'd had the advantage of inspecting some impressive fall flora in the fields near the old Bowl as we waited for the light to change again and again and again. Apparently, nature does very well without fretting over the Ivy League standings.

We asked two traffic directors for the route to Parking Lot D. The first said, "One left and three rights," which 25 minutes later brought us back to where we started. The second said, "Three lefts," which, it turned out, was an excellent plan because 50 minutes later, after the bumper-to-bumper sojourn into West Haven and back, we reached a spot in Parking Lot D at 1:46 p.m., nearly two hours after the game began.

Suzanne, however, reminded me, "Look, the only part of this game that really matters is the last five minutes." I didn't know it at the moment, but her gridiron wisdom would be confirmed.

At about this time, she received a text from a friend who has been on the faculty of both schools involved in the day's fracas. It said, "Go Harvard, or Yale."

I had been a stranger to The Game, though I had been to

the Bowl many times. And I was surprised to see so many frol-
ickers who may have had little intention of actually watching the
matchup, rather more fixed on shouting hearty "hallos" to old
classmates and tailgating with a variety of libations and, I imagined a little pot. Yale mufflers and sweaters, some looking like they
had been hand knit and a few, perhaps, hand-me-down raccoon
coats were easy to spot although some Harvard crimson letter
sweaters were also worn with pride.

Once inside Bowl grounds, Suzanne and I were reminded
of the enormity of a sports arena first built in 1914 and renovat-
ed nearly a century later, though not quite to the point that we
didn't need to bring pillows (thanks, Suzanne) to put down on
hard benches of Section C, Row 11, Seats 13, and 14, with a strik-
ing view of the northern 25-yard line.

The third quarter was about to begin. We noticed the
Stars and Stripes waving proudly, and it seemed to even flutter
with the beat of the recording of the Village People's "YMCA."
Our flag was sharp and crisp in the blue sky all afternoon.

At the beginning of the third quarter, the scoreboard to
our left was indicating that Harvard led by three points. This was
much less of a disappointment to me than missing the perfor-
mances by the two marching bands, which I suspected had prepared something topical and satirical for the occasion.

But I should at this point offer a thought or two about
the actual action on the field, even though many around us were
talking of other things, such as the stock market, international
affairs, the shocking news out of Wisconsin of the Kyle Ritten-
house trial.

As far as I could tell, number 12 for our side, the quarter-
back, found himself in a state of duress, as if he had no offensive
line to protect him. And, on the Harvard side, they wore amusing
yellow pants. But that's enough expert commentary for the moment. The time was already past 2 p.m., and we were very hungry.

So I went out to see if, on request, I could find a kielbasa for Suzanne, and perhaps a nice veggie sandwich for myself, considering I was in the last classes of cardiac rehab and I didn't want to get a stink eye from the nutritionist.

But when I arrived at the main refreshment stand, there were long lines. Long, unmoving lines. It was as if each customer, once reaching the Promised Land of the counter, in addition to receiving refreshment had reserved fifty minutes of psychiatric counseling. But here's where my fortunes took a turn.

The two young women behind me, chatty and clearly very bright, were exchanging ideas on how, perhaps, to find a way to interpret exactly why there was no line movement. We got to talking, of course. I learned they were third-year law students. And one of them, a researcher extraordinaire, had done menu reconnaissance and reported that, alas, no kielbasa or kale were available.

In our time waiting, they asked me questions about myself. Which is odd in a Yale setting. That is, in such a place, the usual conversation among strangers involves an impressive gushing of self-reference without once uttering, "Tell me something about yourself." These young women were actually interested in learning about other people. Perhaps I should have guessed, then, the revelation that came next.

They informed me that they couldn't comfortably reveal, given the circumstances, exactly where they go to law school.

But—hint, hint—it's not in New Haven. They had arrived on a chartered bus from Cambridge.

And these two bright, compassionate young people were aware at this point that my desire to fetch whatever food was available and get back to portal 17 outweighed my wish to stand in line until the spring thaw. So, one of them said, "Tell us what you'd like, and we'll bring it to you."

"What?" I thought. Isn't this a twist—two daughters of

John Harvard demonstrating mercy to a Yale lecturer? I took out my wallet to give her some cash, but they refused to take it.

As one explained, after she saw the message on my hat, "Vietnam Veteran," that, "It's the least we can do for you, as you've done so much for us." She took a photo of my seat location, and said, "We'll do our best."

I told Suzanne this remarkable story when I returned and saw on the scoreboard that each team had scored a touchdown, and that the Harvards were still three points up. So I hadn't missed anything.

Number 12 for our side was still getting harassed to the point of Geneva Convention violations when he tried to pass. And number 19, the QB for the foul side, wasn't faring much better.

This concludes the part of the tale meant to dispense definitive color commentary. Except that, evading his pursuers, number 12 heaved a long pass down the right sideline to a fleet fellow in blue who caught the ball and ran to the end zone. Our side was ahead with only a few minutes to go. "Bulldog! Bulldog! bow wow wow!"

At this point, the two Harvard law students arrived at Row 11 looking for us. They had food, and once again I pulled out my wallet to send a $20 bill down the row but they shook their heads, and passed two hot dogs and a large bottle of Coke, the original kind, which I last drank probably in 1986. It tasted great. And so, too, the hot dogs, which we had read recently in the *New York Times* would take 36 minutes off each of our lives. Worth it.

The football gods must have noticed this act of Harvard charity, as they rewarded the Crimson with a last-minute touchdown, and therefore The Game.

But as we exited the bowl, we saw not a single tear shed in the departing crowd. It was as if people had barely noticed

"Lost?" "Really?" "Was there a game?"

We found our car in Parking Lot D, and drove out. Amazingly, it seemed as if every car driven in from Korea or Japan or Sweden or Italy had already departed for foreign shores. The ride home across town to East Rock was swell, and we congratulated ourselves on a sparkling, if not entirely winning, adventure.

Happy Hour at the Dog Park

On the way to the dog park one early afternoon, I watched a speeding car hit a highway barrier and spin in a 360-degree revolution. The driver, one of many daft people at the wheel of late, managed to total only his sedan and not any eyewitnesses. Then he crept off to the exit on his rims, smoke billowing from the hood, and succeeded in reminding all of us how close we come every day to profound misfortune.

On the way to the dog park one early morning, the first November frost became apparent. And at the park itself, this caused a stir among those of us who figure, if our calendar math is correct, it will be a long time until the spring without even the prospect of flying to Florida on Avelo, the new airline that saved Tweed from irrelevance.

On the way to the dog park one late afternoon, I snapped off the news on the radio, frustrated by the bunkum coming out of the nation's capital, and by general American mendacity. As much as Covid-19 became a pandemic, so did the disease of rampant hostility. Even a reader of the New Haven Independent can see the enmity in some reader comments under many pieces.

But at the dog park on these days and so many others, I see a different society. No sooner do these four-legged creatures get to the gate when they demonstrate their devotion to living in the moment, shutting out the past and future. Finding in every fellow creature delight and adventure, and nothing else but now.

It's as if they all heard the Colin McEnroe show on WNPR on the subject of nothing. And the power of nothing. Unless it's something. Or some such, if I understood anything.

"What are you so happy about?" I yell to Lucca. But he does not respond. He is in a state of constant pleasure at any of the parks we visit, even when a ruffian—and there are a few of these—knocks him over or nips at his floppy ears or humps him, which, after all, is only fair as he has become something of a master at that public obscenity.

My fault, of course. My failure as a trainer. Actually my wife's failure. (Just kidding, Dear.) To be sure, I do admonish this little Italian pooch for such behavior. But he doesn't sulk.

He doesn't decide, in that muffin-shaped noggin of his, "Boy, have I had it unfairly lately. Meals cut from three to two each day on the advice of my veterinarian, and having her stick that stupid light into my ears to see if they're still infected." Lucca doesn't threaten to bring a lawsuit complaining that I only throw the ball for him to fetch 925 times a day instead of the preferred 1,000. He just plays.

The playmates are legion. I would list the breeds, or the mixtures, but I am a novice at this canine stuff, getting a dog, by the evidence, only once every 77 years. What I do know is rampant joy when I see it. And I have to go to the dog park to find it.

Lucca runs as if he is a thoroughbred, though he doesn't measure up compared to some quicker dogs. As the cranky but quotable 1950s manager of the Yankees, Casey Stengel, used to say about a slow player, "He runs too long in one place."

Meanwhile, back in the human sector, the dreaded Covid business has gone to our heads, has cramped us, has knocked us off our stride.

Losing our access to art and reason, we have also mislaid a sense of common humanity amid political insanity responsible for the loss of tens of thousands of lives.

I have tried, with little success, to argue that America has seen inanity and revolution before and survived. Most of my peers are convinced, and for apparently good cause, that it is better now to be an old person — and suffer the demeaning forces of aging — than to be among those youngsters who will inherit our mess.

In the crazy world, only our pets fear none of this. In Lucca's head there is only, "I'm hungry, but maybe the tongue of this shoe will sate me," and "Let's go to the dog park."

Unlike me, he didn't have to drive three times a week to cardiac rehab, on the way perhaps being stung by a driver whose license should have been stripped years ago, or having to endure the endless posturing of evil men and women in "public service."

He is just Lucca, who has dozens of pals and no fear of the future. As a Russian spy in a John LeCarre novel replied, when asked if he is worried about what will happen to him when he is found out, "Worry? Would it help?"

I admit here that I'm showing my own intolerance even as I argue for less of it. But then, as in other measures, not all intolerance is equal. Some is intended to rip us apart, to undermine the values that make our form of government, economy and way of life possible.

And while I'm at it, I'll admit, too, that canines, for whatever their merits, have never developed life-saving vaccines or created great art. What they have done, however, is remind us of the value of carpe diem.

So, today, go out to the people park. Breathe the bracing air. And say something tolerable to someone. Tomorrow can wait.

Up the Rock

On a Sunday morning in early October, with the weather too reasonable to allow another day frittered away inside with political complaint, my wife Sue suggested we improve our sense of wellbeing with a walk to the top of East Rock.

In many local households, such an urging would not make news. East Rock, looming a mere 366 feet above the neighborhood named after this 20 million-year-old basalt deposit, has been hiked, biked, driven up, and otherwise ascended by tens of thousands over the years. It's such an institution that its famous Giant Steps portion, the shortest route upwards, was enhanced with new railings as recently as December of 2020.

So, reader, why should you care about the three hours that Sue and I spent scaling, resting, derailing and depleting ourselves on that day? You shouldn't, except that certain human discoveries may enlighten that had nothing to do with my distressed old legs.

I believe, of course, in omens. Who doesn't? So it seemed only apt that early in the adventure I saw coming the other way my very own gastroenterologist. Though she didn't say so when we chatted briefly, she must have been surprised to see me out there, considering that in our latest conversation, via video conference, we lamented a lab test that verified my considerable case of anemia. I had looked up possible treatments, and saw no verifiable suggestions that seniors who suffer from anemia can cure themselves through self-induced exhaustion.

About forty minutes later, after Sue and I had made some use of stairways, we emerged on the main road upward, and were met by two middle-aged (at least) fellows coming down after reaching the summit and the Civil War monument atop it. For a second, I had a flashback to the days I used to run the Chester Four on the Fourth every Independence Day. I was not terrible at it, often finishing the course in front of the ambulance, and once just ahead of an 80-year-old woman running barefoot. But I always was envious, midway through when the leaders and even some men or women pushing baby buggies headed for the home stretch while I still had two miles ahead of me. Up there on East Rock, the two men we met gleefully pointed out we still had a mile and half to go to the top.

At this point, I said to Sue that I couldn't do it. Never mind that as an ROTC recruit in the early '60s I embarked on forced marches of many miles and survived them all, despite my bone spur. This old body, though bolstered by excellent instruction by our Pilates professor, produces so many irritations these days that when someone asks me how I feel I have to stop and consider the hierarchy of aches, because otherwise I might not notice them.

Still, what choice do we have. Sue said, "Look, we've been saying for five years we'd climb this thing. We're almost there. We shouldn't quit now." I nodded my head instead of saying, "Really, dear, if I have to go to my grave without ever completing this and my tombstone says, 'A competent fellow otherwise, he gave up in his attempt to climb East Rock."

We persisted, though stopped at a point where the rock once again shot straight up and Sue pretended, for the sake of a photograph, to be a rock climber (which is not legal here). I posted the photo on Facebook, and within minutes some friends warned that she had stuck her hands in poison ivy.

Ninety minutes after we had started, we reached the top. If we were delighted by our triumph, we also shared it with many other people who did not look exhausted and did not rest in prone position on a park bench as we did. Some of these people had little kids in hand, none of whom seem to be shouting, "This is child abuse. I'm calling the authorities."

No, climbing to the top is not worthy of the old "Wide

World of Sports" program, with the thrill of victory or as in this case, the agony of da feet. It's just a private, if very good feeling, that we'd accomplished something.

From the summit, of course, one can see all of New Haven. The Pearl Harbor bridge seems to have toy cars on it. Yale seems sufficiently ivied. Long Island Sound is not far off. And the park below began to show its October glories. It was a moment, certainly, to thank not only our bodies and minds for making this adventure so worthwhile but also those local activists in the early 1960s who successfully objected to the original plans for I-91 that would have split East Rock Park in two and otherwise demolished the peace of a beautiful neighborhood.

What I hadn't figured was that the way down would prove to have its own challenges. I wanted to take the shortest way down, but Siri on my GPS seemed entirely confused. "In 180 feet, turn right," she said. But that would mean, literally, "walk off a cliff." Then she corrected herself, "Turn left in 360 feet," and then "turn right in 90 feet," and "turn left (now)," and so on. She is not good at dizzying heights. And so we retraced our steps, going back the way we came. We met a young couple on the way. The fellow noticed my veterans hat and mentioned that he, too, had just served in the Army, most recently in Korea.

This reminded me of my idea for the Pentagon, which so far has gained no support. That instead of sending young men to be in harm's way, the United States should send people like me. For one thing, they'd only need to fund a one-way ticket, as we'd never make it back. For another, they'd help solve the Social Security crisis if enough of us didn't survive. But as I say, as sensible as this suggestion is, no authority has seen fit to act on it.

Midway down the trail, my legs seemed to be giving out. Sue, meanwhile, was well ahead of me in her usual confidant stride. I wanted to yell, "Take the Giant Steps down," as that might cut off the trek by a few yards, but didn't seem to have the energy. I passed couples running up the trail, and a broad-chested fellow who dropped to the ground to do push-ups. What in hell?

When we got back down on level ground another man, in our age group, was on hands and knees at the edge of the road, and we asked, "Are you okay?" He said that he was, but that he had lost his binoculars and was trying to find them. He was apparently using them to spot much in the way of the abundant flora and fauna along the route. It was an odd moment, but it did remind me of the convenient access we all have to what can, if not cure us of our ailments, at least remind us that we are part of a world that is much more enriching than CNN would show us.

When we returned home, we were too tired to make lunch. I lay down on the couch and turned on a football game. I saw a bunch of men running around and smashing into each other. I thought, "Well, guys, enjoy it while you can." And, thought of Churchill, or was it Twain, who said, "Whenever I have the urge to exercise, I sit down and wait for the urge to pass."

Ode to an Ill-Fated Pharmacy

I watched from across the street as a young man walked up to the front door of an abandoned East Rock storefront and tried to peek through the shaded windows. Where, he must have wondered, was the drug counter, the mini-post office, the usual human bustle?

The fellow was, by then, one of hundreds of neighborhood denizens who yet hadn't heard the dyspeptic news that our independent drug store had closed for good. East Rock Pharmacy, after all, had stood at the corner of Orange and Linden streets since 1909.

Its latest owners in the historic Hall Benedict building held onto the crazy idea that in the Age of CVS, Walgreens, Walmart, Stop & Shop, etc., that it was still possible for a little pharmacy to survive. And survive it did, until Thursday, August 30, 2018, when I went in during the final hours to see if I could score one last 90-day supply of a medicine that eases my swallowing.

But swallow this development? My wife and I had boasted about our perfect Rockwellian setting, our condo on Orange, where we walk to the gym, East Rock Park, Italian markets, the coffee shop where a klatch has met every morning over many years, the wine store, our corner Italian restaurant, places that peddle tongue-burning chicken wings and thin-crust pizza, the wellness center and, should we get the urge, an office to have dental implants installed. It seemed to us that the way this retro neighborhood was going, and with handy public transportation to downtown, we could soon become a no-car family.

At this, there have been only guesses as to what will replace what's gone at Orange and Linden, but surely no pharmacy business would sacrifice its health by filling it. Online suggestions range from a place of refreshment (a gelateria) to one that specializes in herbal remedies to one in which certain substances would be sold that would raise fierce objections from certain political quarters.

Cannabis or not, we nevertheless will continue to feel loss. Indeed, in our case we forged a close connection to the pharmacy the very week we moved to New Haven from Chester.

We ordered a prescription and, because it was a frigid night, we took advantage of the pharmacy's delivery service though we live only two blocks away. We expected our package at about 6 p.m., but at 7:30 it still hadn't arrived. Perhaps, we thought, this was a scam. We were new to the neighborhood, and perhaps the folks at the pharmacy said to each other, "Aha. Suckers have just moved in. Do they think it's 1953, and the egg man and the milkman come to the door every day?"

Well, weren't we surprised when we got a call from the deliverer who said he was at our place. We went to the door but saw no one there. "You're kidding," I said to the man on the phone. "You're invisible."

"No, sir," he said. "I'm not getting any answer to my ring."

"Where exactly are you?" I asked.

"Your house in Chester, sir." Forty miles away.

No. This was no scam. East Rock Pharmacy was a place of little miracles, where the people behind the counter knew your name, and were happy to work with chain stores when you found yourself, say, in Washington, D.C., and discovered that you left your Levothyroxine, 100 milligrams, back in New Haven, and were worried that your delicate medical condition would prevent you from joining the protest in Lafayette Park against, well, you name it.

The pharmacy wasn't perfect, of course. No place is. You couldn't access medications online. Its prices for grooming needs were higher than in the chains. And, in the end, it bungled its closing, giving customers little notice, saying only that the employees would retreat to the company headquarters in Wallingford to focus on the long-term care market, and even then sending a confusing message about which pharmacy would inherit their retail business.

Early indications were that the CVS on Church Street was the go-to substitute. But then it appeared that it was the CVS on Whalley Avenue that was chosen. Indeed, the latter was the preferred place because it has a parking lot and a drive-through window.

Just like the suburbs. Ugh.

Perhaps, though, the last word on this should go to our late U.S. poet laureate Donald Hall, who grew up in Hamden and was related to the folks who began the Hall Benedict business. Here, then, is appropriate advice from "Poem Beginning With a Line From Wittgenstein:"

The world is everything that is the case,
Now stop your blubbering and wash your face.

A Very New Haven Birthday

A decade-long study from the National Institute for Redundant Information has found there are three ways to celebrate a birthday in the United States:

1. Have a party.

2. Pass the occasion quietly because you are not inclined to advertise that you are a year older.

3. Be surprised by your devoted spouse and asked to pack an overnight bag and go off into downtown New Haven for a day and night and morning of revelry.

This last was the position in which I found myself in November 2018.

Suzanne had put a great deal of thought into the celebration, knowing that downtown New Haven is the most happening urban spot in Connecticut. What one entrepreneur — a native of Philadelphia who announced plans to bring Philly cheese steaks to Chapel Street — calls "The Heartbeat of Connecticut."

We Ubered from our East Rock neighborhood to The Study on Chapel Street, a highly rated lodging and a quintessential stop for visiting scholars, performers, and, apparently, birthday boys. (Just recently, we spotted Supreme Court Justice Sonia Sotomayor and actor Bradley Whitford in its environs.) As we checked in, I wore my Vietnam vet hat, and, as it was the same week as the Veterans Day holiday, Suzanne secured a discount for our stay.

The second-floor room featured a bathroom with accommodations for the handicapped, which, of course, I could have viewed, if I were more paranoid than I already am, as a comment on my stage of life.

As we had a couple of hours before dinner, we uncorked the bottle of Champagne that Suzanne brought, and, wrapped in the luxurious bathrobes, we jumped under the covers. I had thought about walking a few blocks, perhaps to the Institute Library to get lost in the stacks of classic books, but instead I took up my passionate hobby of napping.

Our dinner reservations were for 8 p.m. but by 6:30 we were hungry and pushed the reservation up. The hostess in The Study dining room led us to a seat next to a gentleman dressed in the old professorial manner: woolen suit, vest, and tie.

He was, I dare say, of an age more advanced than mine, which these days is some trick.

When, for example, I show up at Sprague Auditorium for a concert or Yale Rep for a play, I spend several minutes scouting for signs of people who consider me a mere child, and only on lucky nights am I able to spot a few.

We ordered extravagantly — it was my birthday — though when choosing our wine, once again demonstrated the difficulties of a mixed marriage.

Suzanne likes white and I red, and this has proven one of life's greatest exasperations. It is impractical to order a bottle of anything to share, as it isn't economical or sensible. But on this night, hey, my wife, who is a published poet, and everyone knows that poets make more money than the combined income of Bill Gates and Jeff Bezos, was paying the bill. So, "Bring on the Barolo, the Sancerre, the Screaming Eagle."

After a while, we noticed that the older gentlemen next to us was not waiting for anyone but dining alone. My wife commented to me that he had, in her mind, placed the perfect order, and she was annoyed that she had not done so herself: a dry martini, straight up, a shimmery platter of gelatinous oysters, and a rare filet of beef followed by three scoops of ice cream for dessert.

As we are a gregarious couple we set about to say, "Good evening." This step, of course, violates Connecticut's "None of Your Business" laws, even if the parties in question are only separated by the width of the waiter's behind. But when you reach a certain age, you feel you have earned a license to cross these boundaries. After all, we had a president in Washington who didn't want to be inconvenienced by such trivialities as criminal acts. "Good evening," the gentleman responded, unafraid to engage in social niceties.

He explained without a prompt that he was retired from Yale, and that he was a former dean. I did not think it was wise, considering his exalted CV, for me to explain my two minimal connections with Yale at the time: That I had heard of the place, and that for several summers I have been on the faculty of the Yale Writers Workshop, a position far less demanding and distinguished than the work he had done. So our conversation ended without further interrogation. *Bon appetite!*

Suzanne and I ordered a chocolate extravaganza for dessert that I was certain would counteract the Trazadone prescription that I take nightly to help me sleep. I imagined a headline in the New Haven Independent: "New Haven Man Dies on His Birthday from an Overdose of Contentment."

The next day, we went to breakfast at Atticus, where the menu is inventive and where they still sell things called books.

We were fueled, then, and ready for a full morning at the Louis Kahn-designed Yale Center for British Art, where we hadn't visited since it had closed for remodeling.

The museum's present feature was a stunning exhibit of paintings by George Shaw, celebrated for his stark depictions of the banality of English suburbs. We spent more time than we planned in the galleries, and because we did, an inevitable event took place: As we were leaving, we ran into old friends who live in Deep River and who were there to see the same exhibit. The bespoke bicycle maker Richard Sachs and his wife, the Kirkus book reviewer Deb Paulson, were celebrating Deb's birthday.

Apparently, great Nov. 13 minds think alike. We made

plans to meet for lunch at, where else, the Union League Cafe, where such mutual occasions can be celebrated over Champagne, and near the fireplace.

By the time lunch was over — it was exquisite, just as the company, although the waiter seemed to have a cold, a circumstance that, considering my new age, gave me the willies — we had been gone from the house on Orange Street for nearly twenty-four hours but it seemed like a fine forever.

I thought about how lucky I was to be married to such a woman who would learn, even before the National Institute for Redundant Information, of the value of a New Haven birthday. I tried to return the birthday favor.

In October of the next year, we were in Syracuse, N.Y., for a book event scheduled at Syracuse University, where the artist Sol LeWitt, the subject of my biography, had earned a bachelor of fine arts degree in 1949. Not knowing the city, I made a reservation at the most expensive restaurant listed on Tripadvisor.

When the Uber driver unexpectedly brought us to an enormous shopping mall for Suzanne's birthday dinner, I began an entire evening of apologies. This was a chain restaurant that specialized in delivering many pounds of red meat to every table, and in our case long before the glasses of white and red wine arrived.

We looked out over the décor and atmosphere, and discovered that, through the front window and under the pounding Muzak, we had an unobstructed view of the Beef Jerky Outlet. My only consolation was that soon we'd be heading back to New Haven, and Suzanne would forget about the disgrace of it all. Which she may have until I brought it up again here.

Piano Peace

On a day in late summer, I walked past a house near my own and heard the strains from a piano. It was a real acoustic keyboard, of the pre-electronic kind.

And it set me off on two adventures, one mental and one physically intrusive.

The person inside the house played well but became stuck on a passage from Mozart's "Rondo Alla Turca" (or "Turkish March"), practicing those bars over and over, as one must do when stuck.

This piece, to play it properly, requires some flying fingers, grace notes, muscle memory, a peppery pedal and, of course, discipline.

I had played it as a kid, and remembered how it may have convinced my teacher that my efforts over nine years of lessons might be all for naught.

Miss Fessler was old school. She insisted that her students play the right notes in the right way, paying attention to accents, phrase markings, crescendos and diminuendos, and proper tone. In short, obstacles that diminish the prospects of most would-be prodigies.

Each December, though, she delivered delight. Driving her green Studebaker to our house for my Tuesday afternoon lesson, she brought books of Christmas music. Which meant I could put aside Mozart, Clementi, and other frenzied note-makers to play carols, much easier to learn. This annoyed my mother no end.

It irked her that she had to purchase each book (about $4 at the time, plus the fiver for the lesson) and didn't think her Bar Mitzvah boy should be so enchanted by "O Holy Night."

I argued that many great Christmas songs were written by Jews — among them Irving Berlin ("White Christmas"), Johnny

Marks ("Rudolph, the Red-Nosed Reindeer"), Jay Livingstone ("Silver Bells") and it was Mel Torme who penned the line, "Chestnuts roasting on an open fire."

She went to her default argument: "Just because somebody else jumps into the lake, you're going to jump in the lake, too?" To which I replied, smartly, "Huh?"

Soon after the new year, Miss Fessler and I returned to the usual fare, and I had to practice hard for the spring recital at the teacher's Victorian house. There, a dozen girls in sundresses and one boy in an itchy brown woolen suit sipped tea and then each of us played our respective recital piece to proud parental ears.

Mine one year was that "Rondo." During my next private lesson, my teacher said, "You know, as far as your piano skills go, you should take up the bass fiddle."

This was Miss Fessler's Germanic way of delivering hard truths. And it is true that although I ignored her advice and have continued to tickle the ivories for seven decades, my name has never appeared on a program at the Horowitz Piano series at Yale's Sprague Memorial Hall. At least I don't think so.

But, ah yes, that Turkish march being played recently by an East Rock neighbor. I tried to imagine if it was a man or a woman or a kid at the keyboard. How heavy was the touch, how graceful were the notes? This I knew was a fruitless inquiry, as talent is talent and pays no attention to age or gender.

I thought, "I think I'll just knock on the door and give that person a pointer or two about difficult passages." But the player did not stop practicing to welcome me in.

Perhaps on hearing my knock, the musician thought, "Oh, I get it. Using the ruse of door-to-door Mozart advisor, an old man worms his way into the house and steals my rare sheet music copy of Gene Autry's 'Back in the Saddle Again.'"

So, my help rejected, I just kept walking, and forgot about my little musical interlude until I recently saw the new film "The

Power of the Dog," set in 1925 in Montana, in which Benedict Cumberbatch plays the lead role of a Yale grad in the classics who has gone west and gone rogue.

Without giving anything of plot substance away here, I'll reveal that sometime in the first half of the film, a baby grand arrives at the ranch. It's a Mason & Hamlin, built in Boston, the same brand and size that I have, and probably built around the same time as mine, which was 1913.

A big deal is made out of it in the film, as I have made a big deal out of mine, which I bought in 1988 from the superb piano rebuilder Shawn Hoar in West Hartford.

I had a 100th birthday party for the Mason a few years ago as a fundraiser for our Chester synagogue, and I asked Dan Pardo, who was associate music director at the Goodspeed Opera House, to play a tune composed in every decade of the piano's life.

So we went from ragtime to Gershwin to Samuel Barber to Billy Joel and rap to a piece with lyrics of my own, the title song of the musical, "A Woman of a Certain Age." Ninety minutes and many hors d'oeuvres after we began, we had raised $6,000.

I also had the pleasure of improvising on the 88 in a jazz combo, and providing oom-pahs for a Klezmer band. (Take *that*, Miss Fessler.)

Lately, I've been trying to master and memorize the haunting theme from the HBO series, "Succession." I'm encouraged. At the rate I'm progressing, I'll have it down pat, provided I live another 62 years.

On the other hand, there is something intoxicating about the power and subtlety of the old Mason. Sometimes I just get lost in it. I play the melody and harmony to the Jimmy Van Heusen/ Johnny Burke love ballad, "It Could Happen to You," and then, unexpectedly, I hear my wife Suzanne's lovely voice.

"All I did was wonder how your arms would be, and it happened to me."

The magic of music—music we can make ourselves or swipe from those who really know how, to try to play the same notes that Beethoven or Duke Ellington composed and performed themselves, well, that's a balm for these times.

By the way, this piece is not a pitch to teach you to play the piano for considerably more than a fiver a week. But maybe the bass fiddle.

Goodbye (Again), Columbus

She asked, "Are you American?" I wasn't sure she was talking to me. Perhaps someone behind me. But there was no one behind me, as we sat spaced apart in a tent outside of a complex of personal service shops, both of us awaiting our turn to enter one or the other.

"I am an American," I said.

"I'm interested in your opinion then." I could hear a heavy Eastern European accent in her voice, noted that her hair had just been colored jet black, and that she appeared to be as old or older than me, which is a rarity these days.

She asked, "What do you think about the Columbus statue?"

"Hmm," I said. I hadn't anticipated being grilled on the subject as I awaited a socially distant pedicure. But of course, Columbus was, and had remained, a subject of consuming interest locally ever since authorities decided to remove a statue of the explorer from Wooster Square.

She did not wait for me to get around to answering. "I think it's crazy," she said.

"What's crazy?" I asked.

"To take down the statue. To erase the history."

At that point, I had a choice. One instinct, short-lived, was to engage in the matter on its merits. To say something like, "I can see both sides of the issue." Yes, that would have probably sufficed, gotten me through the moment, though I abhor the 50-50 approach. Nothing is 50-50, particularly the odds that a person of a mature age can get through these days without being summoned to testify in the Court of Moral and Cultural Affairs.

I could have said, "We all know of the discrimination that Italians faced when they came to America," and that the statue represents more than Columbus's achievements in his four voyages to the new world. And that it was remarkable for its time — built and financed in 1892 by an oppressed community of immigrants in a time when only the statues of "real Americans" were common. "People of Italian heritage point with pride to the legacy."

Or I might have said, "Well, the legacy is a tough one, really." But what would have been the point of going into the many witnesses on Hispaniola who charged Columbus with serious crimes while governing the island, including the cutting out of tongues, dismemberment, murder, and other inhumane summary judgment?

I decided instead, as I often do, just to listen, for that has been important over the decades to the work I do as a writer. I knew the temperature of our conversation would revert to normal if she talked a while, and I could hear her reasons.

I was curious. Why would a woman from the Czech Republic (she revealed this at some point during the conversation) have such a deep feeling about the Columbus statue? I wanted to know. And, in the next few minutes, I actually learned something — a gift that often arrives in the heart of a patient listener, though patient listening has been a casualty of our times.

I had been on edge that afternoon, having viewed earlier the video made by the New Haven Independent of a confrontation in Wooster Square between two Black Live Matter protesters and a group of Italian-American men that turned ugly, and that contained perhaps a record number of f-bombs hurled in various directions, and some pushing, shoving, punching, attempts to reason, and, in the end, a partial reconciliation.

"Is what happened in the square a microcosm of America?" I asked myself, and was tempted to answer in the affirmative.

But there is nuance in play if the noise doesn't drown it out, and there are deep feelings that reflect no "both sides" tolerance.

The woman from the Czech Republic, after no prodding from me, talked of living her formative years under Communism, and that made the subject of freedom one that supersedes all else. We talked of the rebellion in Hungary in 1956, when Soviet tanks plowed through downtown Budapest, and of outrages closer to her home.

She said that when she thought of America in the years that followed that she had a hero, an actual modern-day savior. That was President Ronald Reagan, "who stood up to the Soviet Union and freed us."

At that point, of course, I had another choice. I could express my own view of Reagan, much less charitable, and explain why, or I could actually take in what the woman was saying, and try to understand from her point of view how the 40th president became a godsend to the people living under soul-numbing oppression.

I easily chose the latter, and no doubt this choice was influenced by our own collective experiences in the Trump years, when truth was turned into fiction and when non-whites have seen a return of blatant racism and oppression (voting rights and other basic freedoms) from top levels of the government.

But still, the question of Columbus remained to be solved. Why was she so determined to defend a man who brought suffering to so many?

There has been a move afoot lately, of course, to lump all statues of controversial men (and so far, all men), in one category, and to say the honor of being recognized in perpetuity in the public square should be limited to angelic figures, of which, at last count, there are none. Even the saintly Mother Teresa has taken hits of late.

However, Ronald Reagan, to my new Czech acquaintance, is an angelic figure. To her, if there were a thousand statues around the land of "the Gipper," it wouldn't be enough. He is not the president that denied relief and empathy at the start of the AIDS epidemic or whose "Reaganomics" discriminated against the poor.

There are hundreds of honors for Columbus in this country, and for Italian-Americans that number, too, may not be enough. The Czech native seemed to understand that. For she is not one, understandably, to weigh all issues and to render balanced judgment. She was a victim, just as Italian-Americans were victims, and then she became free, just as they did.

Many commentators argue persuasively that the excesses and cruelties of our traditional heroes are not relative, a product of their time. They are instead real, and cruel, and should be recognized as such. Slave owners were never enlightened, because they kept human beings in captivity. Yet each of us, reflecting not only on our own histories but the histories of our fellow citizens of the world, need to show empathy, to listen, and to reach our own informed conclusions about honor and disgrace.

As the Czech immigrant and I ended our foray into recent and not-so-recent history, and a staffer from the nail salon summoned me to come in, my partner in conversation said she enjoyed our brief time together and wished me good luck. I returned the sentiments.

Then, as I walked away, she shouted, "Young man!"

Young man? Indeed a compliment. "You forgot your water bottle."

How to Sell a Used Subaru

Step One: You sign up in the fall of 1961 for a college course called Introduction to ROTC, because, though you have no urgent desire to shoot anyone, you are a child of World War II.

Step Two: Four semesters later, you face a decision. Recovered from your first clinical depression after spending too much time acting in plays and writing features for the campus daily while neglecting to go to classes, you are given a choice: enroll in the advanced curriculum of the art of war, or drop out of the study of war. If you stick with it, you must report for active duty after graduation, something distasteful. If you don't, you'll probably be drafted, something distasteful. But you are far from alone in this conundrum. This is because this is the fate of most young men who in the Cold War era had the misfortune to experience excellent health. And, as the son of a veteran who didn't rise above staff sergeant in the Pacific, you'd rather begin your own military stint with a commission. Or, in military lingo, "an officer and a gentleman." Besides, there seems to be no Hot War at the moment. So you opt to stay, in part because the Pentagon bribes you with payments of twenty-seven dollars per month, enough to cover your laundry bill and Sunday editions of the New York Times, which your international relations professor requires you to read, as he expects you to grasp why the world is a perpetual powder keg, and why politicians don't understand anything, although that doesn't stop them from expressing their ignorance and sending young people to their deaths before going off on their golf outings at the Congressional Country Club.

Step Three: You receive, along with your bachelor's of science in journalism sheepskin, a commission in the United States Army in the Quartermaster Corps, which relieves you, as it is a "non-combat branch." You drive your Dodge Dart, the one you bought new for $1,976 because it was heavily dented in a hailstorm, to the American South for training and your permanent duty station, which turns out to be permanent for six months. During that time, you serve as commissary store officer, explaining to customers why the price of a gallon of whole milk has jumped from thirty-one cents to thirty-three cents though you don't really have a clue. And you are also given the additional duty of assistant mortuary officer, which turns out to be something of an omen.

Step Four: Because you have no say in the matter, you embark on an all-expenses- paid voyage to a gorgeous landscape of the southern part of Vietnam that, unfortunately, is home at the moment and for years afterward to vile circumstances. There, in a country fatally divided by politics, religion, colonialism, revenge, hard economic realities, and landmines, many of your fellow soldiers, fighting a war that will be torn asunder by historians, are sent home in body bags, and many others will face years or decades of mental consequence. Your "noncombat branch" is suddenly the target of ambushes. As the convoy commander, you barely escape one of them because the AK-47 round aimed at your brain rips instead through the jeep's canvas top. (Had the sniper's aim been slightly better, he would have obviously rendered you ineligible to write this account.) Yet, against expectations, you survive your own eleven-month, thirteen-day, six-hour, twenty-three-minute tour with no serious physical traumas.

Step Five: You return to civilian pursuits, a member of a disgraced society of veterans of the most controversial war since that mess started at Fort Sumter, and follow your nose for news as a newspaper writer and Sunday magazine editor. The war is officially over, but, unofficially, it becomes the source of nightmares so prevalent that you can't ever leave it in the past. In these nighttime skirmishes, you are ordered to return to Vietnam to do it right this time. But your boots are missing. Your insignia, too.

And your fatigue pants. You reply to the commanding officer, "I'd like to go back to war, but I have nothing to wear." In real life, from your editor's desk, you publish stories of the war that conflict with other stories of the same cataclysm, because no one, not even the sharpest writers and academics (most of whom escaped military service) understand what happened or why, or what the true legacy may be. One story is written by a veteran who ordered an artillery bombardment that, because of his own error in calculating the strike, went astray and killed his best friend. He writes that he sees that friend again every time he goes to sleep, and pleads for forgiveness. In your final decade in the magazine world, you drive a car from your upgraded fleet (a Saab or a top-of-the-line Honda) on the thirty-five-mile commute from your small Connecticut town to the city where you work. One day, your publisher calls and asks you to take on a high school student as an intern. You balk, because all of your interns have been college students. But, as the publisher signs your paycheck, you take on the girl, only sixteen. She is a native of the country that hosted our war, and after it, her father was sent to a re-education camp for many years. Against expectation, the young intern is an instant hit with staff, not only because she brings her mother's pork dumplings to the weekly staff meeting but because she's a human dynamo. She organizes a writers' conference and persuades the likes of Arthur Miller and William Styron to speak. She brims with ideas for profiles and investigations. You become interested in her college plans. She says she dreams of going to Harvard. You ask her what kind of high school grades she gets even though you already suspect they are spectacular, which they are. And how she did on the SATs—a perfect score. You opine that with her academic record, and because she is a member of a segment of the population that such institutions seek to promote campus diversity with, she is a shoo-in. She looks at you as if you are from Pluto. If you knew, she says, how many Vietnamese students score perfectly on the SAT's, you wouldn't say that. In fact, she doesn't get into Harvard, and goes to Brown instead, and studies art, her passion. And years later, goes to law school, and then takes a job in a prestigious firm.

Step Six: In 2010, you buy a used Subaru sedan that has only thirteen thousand miles on it and drive it for seven years. Because your commute is long and your house is isolated in the woods, you and your wife need two cars. She drives a Saab wagon.

Step Seven: Having finished your tour of corporate duty and been granted a buyout in a failing business, you go out on your own as a writer and editor, though a friend advises you not to if you want to be able to pay for car repairs, and, perhaps, groceries. During this time you write some books, and a play about the Vietnam War, though it is not about you but about a childhood friend, a navigator on a fighter jet, whose body was not found for forty years. After the play is staged, friends who see it suggest going back to Vietnam, a step most veterans of the war have avoided.

Step Eight: Because Vietnam has never left you, you decide you will never leave it. And you and your wife, not the wife you were married to in your officer days, because she didn't survive until the end of the war, but your final wife, plan an independent adventure in the place you once feared going to, in order to make sense of things. You discover, in addition to the street food in Ho Chi Minh City, fish stew in Nha Trang, beer in Hue, watermelon in Dalat, and innovative cuisine in the magical village of Hoi An, that the people everywhere are glad to see you. Among your souvenirs: a T-shirt that says "Good Morning, Vietnam."

Step Nine: Because you live an urban life now (you have moved from the little town to a Connecticut city), you and your wife no longer need two cars. So you put the Subaru sedan up for sale, though you don't look forward to the process. Your former intern, the native of Vietnam, whom you've kept in touch with, sees your Facebook pitch and says her brother needs a car in Washington, D.C., and that her mother wants to buy it for him.

Her mother comes to your house a day later, bringing a box of not very Asian homemade doughnuts and a mechanic who is also a native of her home country. He checks the car and says it looks worth the asking price. You take the woman to the Department of Motor Vehicles and wait your six hours until you can transfer the title. The clerk at the window looks at the two of you and might think, well, there's a nice couple. She processes the papers, and all's well.

Step Ten: You sit at the desk in your home office and consider what you thought was once a fine moral to the story of the collective Vietnam experience: that as a country the United States finally would learn from its mistakes and understand the limits of its authority, power, and right to bombard to smithereens other countries so that they can be free. You ask yourself if you are the writer you think you are. Though you've published books before, you never took on, in book form, the best story of your life. You ask, What did that war do to your mind? But by now, of course, having put down these words, you are on your way to figuring it out.

Life at 32 Degrees Fahrenheit

In my defense, there wasn't time that early morning to reflect on the late and beloved forecaster Dr. Mel Goldstein's legacy, or his cheerful warnings about our winter weather.

On the other hand, as I tumbled backwards wondering where I would land and in what condition, even then I understood I should have known beforehand.

When I take the puppy out for his morning "business," as I did on that late December dawn, even he, at the tender age of one year plus, knows to stop and pause at the door to check out nature's promise and obstacles. He does this in the same manner as Dr. Mel did before every appearance on WTNH.

Yes, the good and perpetually smiling doctor had Doppler at his disposal, and all the tools of modern science. Still, as his turn on camera approached he went out on the Elm Street sidewalk, put his finger in the air to test the wind, and looked up at the sky, trusting his own atmospheric perception and instincts. Just as the puppy does.

The native of Massachusetts said that he was drawn to our weather because of the way it so often hovers at the 32-degree mark in winter, which means that the lines between rain, snow and freezing rain are blurred.

We are not, after all, Vermont, where the snow is often dry and fluffy and playful. This makes forecasting in our state difficult, and for seniors (my category), potentially treacherous.

Odd, how so many considerations, memories and regrets flow through the mind in the midst of a tumble backwards.

What had made me think that, in my slippers instead of my old pair of North Face boots, I could maneuver safely up the icy stairs without taking precautions, without having put on the crampons my wife bought for us both.

In this instance, my foolishness led to a circus act without a net. My feet flew up in front of me and I deduced in that moment that the result of such acrobatics would mean my noggin would end up somewhere below where my feet were heading. In this, I proved an excellent forecaster.

BANG. The back of my skull on the left side bounced against the driveway pavement, and even as it did, mind portraits appeared of a scene twenty years ago when I witnessed a young man jaywalking across Middletown's Main Street being hit by a car and thrown to the cement head first. He tried to get up, but then, holding his head in pain, he discovered such a goal was not feasible.

I was luckier. I was not knocked out. My head hurt, of course, but not as much as my left shoulder, which had bounced on the stairs going down. Despite all that was still going on in my consciousness, I didn't yet consider the consequences of this. One never does at such a moment.

What I knew for sure was only that the puppy took an interest in my welfare and pressed his nose against mine, apparently attempting to keep me alive until the EMTs arrived.

This did not happen because, though groggy, I was able to get up, bring him inside, and utter to my wife Suzanne, who had not yet made an appearance from under the bed covers, "YIKES" or words unprintable here.

What followed was a suitable amount of empathy, pity, ice-packing (and irony, no?), Tylenol, steamy oatmeal with raisins and bad television, until the hour arrived when guests came for dinner, and I could enjoy their sympathies.

But seriously, folks, this little tale is meant not only to show my ability to tough it out, a poor measure compared to the way Dr. Mel toughed out all those broadcasts smiling through the pain of multiple myeloma until finally succumbing to his illness in 2012.

It is to warn all fellow seniors of the special challenges of winter for those of us who decided long ago that ice and snow and freezing rain are reasonable substitutes for the considerable hazards of South Florida, and that we are not what we once were.

Stories abound from people we know who have injured themselves, sometimes seriously: fractured arms and legs, concussions, etc.

One friend's account of a broken ankle included, along with a photo of his X-ray, this advice: In general, it's not a good idea to break your ankle.

I'm sure I don't need to bolster this argument with findings from the Mayo Clinic, but just allow a few points made from up in Rochester, Minnesota, which is a world headquarters for serious injury and even death from seniors falling on the ice.

"This is a direct result of aging," says Jeremy L. Fogelson, M.D., and the damage is usually more serious. "Brain blood vessels become more fragile, making them much easier to bleed." Spines and bones, he points out, are more vulnerable, too, in older people.

But somehow we know that already, even if our brains, or at least my brain, still thinks I'm a sturdy fellow.

The Mayo website offers helpful, if obvious, hints as to how to prevent such incidents. These include spreading kitty litter on slippery spots, dressing appropriately [NOT SLIPPERS, you idiot] and even "use a slower and wider gait to better protect against falls."

My goal here, as this tumble tale ends, is to help fellow seniors make it safely through until the spring, when we can find other ways to make ourselves vulnerable to the nature of aging.

Dr. Mel knew the dangers. Nevertheless, his good cheer helped him live on for many years with an illness that was supposed to kill him imminently.

He loved the weather, whatever it was. And I promise to do the same, as I nap near the fireplace.

Stop & Shop & Mutter & Cough

Our city is a profitable place for small businesses, but supermarkets in the city and nearby suburbs still draw heavy traffic, particularly in times of collective terror. Such as when a massive winter storm is expected, and fear spreads that some shopper or other will hoard all the Cheetos. Or more significantly as when, as happened in the spring of 2020, the full force of the Covid-19 pandemic arrived in the Elm City.

We were still many months away from a vaccine, and any news of cures was limited to a president's musings that bleach could do the trick, followed by other extreme and dangerous recommendations from a professional boaster who, whatever his accomplishments, displayed no Yale Medical School sheepskin on his wall.

What to do? Well, panic of course. The disease had already killed hundreds in Connecticut, and local hospitals had to cancel the usual lucrative businesses of elective surgeries in order to address the biggest local and national health crisis in a century. And one business chain, Stop & Shop, announced an idea that, in its view, could surely ease grocery worries.

The pandemic's most vulnerable targets were, in general, the elderly, which last I checked includes people my age who, when asked by medical office workers for our dates of birth, simply reply, "A long, long time ago."

The management of local stores decided to set aside exclusive hours for seniors to shop. It would be carding at its most extreme level. A shopper would have to be sixty years old or older to enter, at 6 a.m., the Stop & Shop store in Hamden, the abutting northern suburb.

At that hour, the store was overrun with customers, the aisles were jammed with traffic, the register lines ran forever, the manager hustled from checkout clerk to checkout clerk trying to speed the cashiering process while seniors queued up as they did in the old days — say, a month earlier — before we knew we were especially at risk for this illness.

Indeed, for a brief period today Hamden became the Clearwater Beach of social distancing. Among the most vulnerable age group, there was almost none.

When pressed by a customer to do something to alleviate the waiting period, the manager replied out of frustration, "I don't have any more cashiers."

When I asked the customer service representative behind the counter, "It doesn't look like a healthy situation, does it?" she responded, "That's probably right."

I spent, in all, about 20 minutes in the frenzy mostly trying not to play bumper cars as at first I loaded up on the onion special (two bags for the price of one, $3.99), some avocados, bananas, cheeses and the like, as I thought of maneuvering to the meat counter to buy packages we could stow back in our New Haven basement freezer.

I dodged men and women wearing masks, some of them bent over their carts.

I thought, "This can't be a good thing."

At that point, I received a text from my Suzanne, who had awakened and realized I had gone off on this adventure after being ambivalent about it last night. (I had watched one of the many medical experts on cable news who warned that seniors should not be tempted by such practices and instead ask juniors to shop for them).

Suzanne listed things we were out of: Mrs. Meyers dishwashing liquid (basil scent), small Glad bags, red kidney beans, cornmeal ("next to the oatmeal," she wrote, helpfully), chicken breasts with the bone in.

When I thought of stocking up on frozen vegetables, memories of childhood ran through my head, though it was only on special occasions when my mother offered Birds Eye rather than canned asparagus and spinach.

But something struck me and stopped me. There was a madness going on. Carts piled over the top, shoppers seemingly desperate, perhaps worried that a food shortage or a shelter-in-place order would deprive us of proper sustenance. The federal government, mostly through its highly regarded medical practitioners, Dr. Trump and Dr. Pence, had assured us this wouldn't be the case, but some of us have come to believe that it isn't always possible to trust what these two experts say.

I texted Suzanne and reported on my observations. She wrote back, "If it's not worth it, come home."

My first thought was to leave my cart and run. But that, too, would be wrong, and I went around and put back all of my purchases in their original places, though I knew that if my hands carried the virus, someone might pick up, say, the Cabot Seriously Sharp Cheddar, and later make a tuna melt with it, not knowing that I'd fingered the thing.

And then I ran. A shopper heading from the overflowing parking lot to the store as I headed out — and warned by me not to go in — replied, "It'll only get worse later, but thanks," as she pushed an empty cart toward the entrance.

The Stop & Shop corporation, to its credit, tried to come up with a plan that would avoid situations such as this morning's boondoggle. Wednesday's Boston Globe quoted a corporate spokesperson on why the new policy is in force every day instead of special days of the week, say Tuesday, Wednesday and Thursday. If the latter were the case, the spokesperson said, "This could result in large crowds, the very situation we are looking to prevent as it will make it more difficult for customers to practice social distancing."

Another Stop & Shop official told the *Washington Post*

this week: "The company doesn't anticipate space between customers as being an issue, considering the size of most stores."

But we are now in a period not only of uncertainty but of widespread danger and fear, and as a result the company couldn't prevent what it feared.

My fellow shoppers had seen a lot of fear and loathing in their lives. Some, older than I (my permanent record goes back only to 1943), had lived through food and gasoline rationing, and the terror of a world war. They had grown up in the era of the polio epidemic, and we can all recall easily the major traumas that followed: the Vietnam War, riots in the cities, the assassinations of inspiring leaders.

And a little more than a month from now, those of us who were on the Kent State campus that spring (I was there to lecture) will mark a half century since the killing of four students and the wounding of 19 others by National Guard troops. Horrible times, all.

Do we build up an immunity to fear and panic as we get older?

I used to think so. But Thursday morning, in the city of Hamden, the evidence didn't support my thesis.

I drove back home, imagining a future without kidney beans, cornmeal, Cabot Seriously Sharp Cheddar. Or perhaps I could come back during the usual Early Bird Special time, say about 4:30 p.m., and jostle with the millennials in the toilet paper aisle.

Hints of Renewed Civilization

A friend who recently moved to East Rock invited us to a dinner party just as the pandemic seemed to be ending. Dinner party? Leave the house? Eat with other people? Change out of my sweatpants?

"Don't worry. All the guests have been vaccinated," she said.

In the interim between invitation and the actual event, I dusted off memories of previous dinner parties in years when attending was not a health hazard, except if the host for the evening was a ghastly cook.

In the summer of 2019, politics became physically threatening. We invited friends to a backyard gathering at our home. It all went well at first.

The Weber grill did its job, the Tuscan wine flowed, laughter was the language of the night, and the weather couldn't have been more accommodating.

It seemed that the evening would end triumphantly. But, well, you know what happens when you think that.

One of the guests was a woman who had charmed us all. And then, out of the fading blue, a friend of hers showed up. He was a big fellow, and seemed congenial, as he took a seat right next to me. But then for some reason, he felt it necessary to indicate the need to reelect the person who then occupied the Oval Office, "the greatest president ever." He then put forward an encyclopedia of conspiracy theories, and the hypothesis that it is people like me who are the real threat to America.

Mind you, he had the audacity to espouse these views right in the heart of the People's Republic of New Haven.

I poured him some Montepulciano in the hopes that alcohol would reduce his fever. But he carried on, and it became necessary for me to speak up, objecting to his points in the most strenuous terms. I did this even though I knew well what Mark Twain had advised: "Never argue with a fool; onlookers may not be able to tell the difference."

This fellow had a broad chest and bulging muscles, and it would have done me no good to challenge him to a fistfight, which I last undertook in the sixth grade with Stanley Zowitz, leading to a painful result.

Fortunately, one of the other guests at the table had mastered the art of talking down even the most ardent of nincompoops. The fellow left without laying a glove on me, and eventually the evening's temperature was lowered.

This, however, was far from the only uncomfortable dinner party. There was, for example, the event Suzanne and I produced as our contribution to a charity fundraiser.

The winning bid of $800 for "Dinner for 8 at 8, Dress to the Nines," was bought by four couples who banded together to come to our house for a formal affair, in which I would play the piano, and Suzanne would serve a truffle-themed dinner. However . . . Because many people were involved, and schedules were complicated, there was some back and forth over the date for the event, and something got lost in the cacophony.

One Saturday night, we were getting ready to retire for the evening after a day in New York when we heard cars pull up in the driveway. Indeed, the four couples had arrived, each dressed, as requested, to the Nines.

One of the women came up the steps carrying a large bouquet of flowers and a ribboned bottle of wine.

"We're so excited," she said. "I know Suzanne is a marvelous cook, and we haven't eaten all day." She then stared up and down, as we were wearing our bed clothes.

"What?" she said. "Is this some kind of a joke?"

In our minds we had planned for the party to occur two

weeks hence, and tried to explain this to our exasperated guests. Not only were we not attired for the occasion but, alas, we'd been away for a few days and there wasn't anything to offer them other than peanut butter and Raisin Bran.

They didn't think that was funny. Nor did we.

In our effort to evade serious scorn, we called around to local restaurants to make a reservation for the eight people. But as it was a Saturday night, not a table could be found. The woman who brought the flowers and wine scooped them up in a huff and left.

When things calmed down a few days later, we established a raincheck date. I put on my tuxedo. Suzanne put on a beautiful dress and filled the champagne flutes on a tray by the front door where we planned to greet them. Candles flickered and fresh flowers had begun to open, as both set a dreamy tableau. The piano was tuned, and I was ready with a new version of Frank Sinatra's 1944 hit "A Lovely Way to Spend An Evening."

They arrived right on time. But when they got out of their cars, we noticed that something was up. None of them were in formal clothes. All had on robes and pajamas.

The joke was on us, and we had a good laugh. Joy reigned once again in Dinner Party Land.

As to last week's event produced by our East Rock neighbor, it turned out that while rust had us all off our games for a few seconds, soon we were back on familiar topics.

It was interesting to see what the guests thought to wear on this occasion. One woman stayed in her "at home for a year" comfort clothes, dark colors, although her husband shone in a blousy orange shirt and Hartford Whalers cap. Our host outshone us all, as she should, also in an orange-ish Indian dress and flowing pants.

In the first few minutes, sitting in the breezy and comfortable back yard for the cocktail hour, we dived right into matters that brought nods of recognition.

One of the guests, an old friend of mine, began a theme that lasted throughout the evening. When we spoke of the pandemic, or Georgia's new oppressive voting law, or how much we have missed the theater and concerts, somehow baseball, which had just started its season, came up.

So, in the same breaths where we mentioned Dr. Jonas Salk or the King of Jordan or, pardon the expression, Congressman Matt Gaetz, there were also interspersed comments about icons of the diamond from our era.

We reviewed the merits of Casey Stengel, Satchel Paige, Marvelous Marv Throneberry, Bill Mazeroski, Yogi Berra, Willie Mays, Al Rosen, and Ted Kluszewski ("The Big Klu") as well as the general consensus around the table that whenever the Yankees lose the pennant, a national holiday should follow.

I was in heaven, especially when we refuted the movie line, "There's no crying in baseball." Some of us recounted crushing moments that reminded us of the old saw, "Baseball is not a matter of life and death. It's more important than that."

Not only was the food wonderful, but I had the occasion, which I always seek, to point out that the Cleveland Indians are Connecticut's home team. That's because it's the Cleveland club, not the Yankees or Red Sox, that plays on land of Connecticut's Western Reserve. (As Casey Stengel often said, you could look it up.)

I poured another glass of wine, and thought: Gee, it's really nice to be back in mid-season form and in civilization again.

On My Tows: A New Haven Revelation

It is something of an achievement that for all of my driving life, I had avoided some of the common pitfalls, including having any of my cars towed, a spotless history beginning with the hail-damaged 1965 Dodge Dart. But this long streak of excellent fortune ended under the glory of a full moon on the evening of September 13 when our 2008 Swedish import disappeared from a lot. Even so, what you will read here is not your typical Saab story. It is, instead, a New Haven revelation.

We were to meet friends from Essex at Skappo, one of our go-to Italian restaurants. Though sometimes when we leave East Rock heading for downtown we hire an Uber, on that Friday night I wasn't in my right mind. I thought, hey, despite the return of faculty and students to Yale and paucity of metered spaces in Ninth Square, I'll choose to do the stupid thing: drive and leave myself at the mercy of the God of Parking.

That way, I'd save a few bucks and, based on previous experience, postpone learning more about the history of Pakistan, Colombia or Lithuania (which I should know anyway, because two of my grandparents emigrated from Vilna, and another from western Russia.)

Indeed, the problem began around the intersection of Orange and Chapel. Inch by inch, we impatiently rued the fact that our city is so exciting at night. As my wife Suzanne and I spent many of our years in Hartford, and its un-electric downtown, we still haven't adjusted to the idea that New Haven sidewalks don't roll up at night.

As I suspected, all metered spaces were taken. Aha, I decided. There is a private parking lot near Skappo, usually unguarded at night. We'd often parked there without incident on Monday nights when we took Italian language lessons from co-owner Anna

Sincavage. Wasn't I clever? Other drivers, though, had been just as brilliant. At least fifteen others. I figured there was safety in numbers.

The dinner was, as usual, a joy. Skappo specializes in Umbrian dishes and good wines, and, on this night, we pressed Anna's daughter, Yvette, to show us pictures of the new member of the family, her son Sebastian, eight months old. Our friends from Essex were only too happy to enjoy the warmth of a place they hadn't been, particularly when Anna emerged from the kitchen with her usual embraces and good cheer.

Over scrumptious meatballs and eggplant, we learned that our friends parked in a public lot for $10, and I thought, well, the naivete of out-of-towners.

After dinner, we said our goodbyes, and before retrieving our car stopped for a moment next door at Firehouse 12 bar to gawk at the great number of young people out on a Friday night. The parking lot still had a few cars in it but not our blue Saab. This was, of course, a disquieting moment. There were only two possibilities. The car was stolen or towed. We noticed a sign at the entrance that said something like: "If you park here illegally you will be towed at your own expense, Lary Bloom."

I called the police department, and the dispatcher reported that our car indeed had been towed — the towing companies must report the details of their victims immediately.

As I often rely on my wife when in a tight spot, Suzanne called the number, and a woman answered. Suzanne, believing that being straightforward with a touch of absurdity is the best practice, asked, "Can you bring the car back?"

The woman laughed, and gave us the location of the lot, 388 Crown. At that point, I was relieved that the usual rules of urban science would apply, among them: Rule 1: The one-way street you need to take is the wrong one-way. Rule 2: If your car is towed on the lower end of Crown Street, you will need to retrieve it at the upper end, a 20-minute walk away.

However, Suzanne and I were cheered by two things. The first was, as she reported, "The fine we'll have to pay might be cheaper than in Manhattan, where I've heard it's $450."

Oh, joy, I thought. The second: We were mesmerized by our city's Manhattan impersonation: people everywhere, restaurants full, sidewalk and motor vehicle traffic aplenty. Even Louis' Lunch had become Louis' Dinner, some people, presumably, learning for the first time there's no ketchup in the place.

Two women dressed to the nines and holding hands walked ahead of us while a fellow clearly impaired from some unsavory substance walked up to them and made some indecent proposal to which they demurred. (As I said, this is city life.)

We walked past College Street, where the entrance was blocked off by barricades. We thought, perhaps, one of those hugely popular rock bands we had never heard of was performing at the College Street Music Hall. But a policeman explained, "It's the Grande Prix bike race, and a street festival, too."

If we had been paying half-attention, we'd have been aware of this. But there is too much to know in our city. When we first moved here from tiny Chester, we rushed to see and hear everything: concerts, lectures, theater. Yo-Yo Ma? You could hear him at Woolsey Hall for $25. Then, exhausted from it all, we retreated to our nights-around-the-fireplace evenings, relying on CNN to bring us into political despair.

Happily, though, a tow truck reminded us that we are alive and well in one of the most eclectic small cities in America.

And no, it didn't cost $450 to be sprung from Crown Street Auto. The tab was $112 hard cash. What a bargain, I thought.

We drove our Saab away, and, at the corner of York and Elm, found ourselves stuck in a 10 p.m. traffic jam as authorities removed barriers from the bike race. And we sat there, in a state of contentment.

Heart Savers: My Time with the Bod Squad

It was to be my final morning at the old brownstone at the corner of Sherman Avenue and Chapel Street.

The building I had driven to every Monday, Wednesday and Friday over a three-month period is where hearts are invigorated, pounds are shed, turnip recipes distributed, and where people who've recently been petrified learn to laugh about life again.

On a December morning, the exercise space on the third floor was filled to capacity—five of us heart patients working hard on our bodies, breathing heavily but happy to be breathing at all.

The location itself provides spiritual uplift. The very tall ceilings, "cathedral" in the authentic sense, marked the upper limits of the Plymouth Congregational Church, built in 1831.

Much later the edifice was sold to a Jewish congregation, Temple Kezer, and lately has been, literally, at the heart of Yale New Haven's cardiac post-op recovery program.

Of the patients going through the hour-long physical workout, I had been through the least invasive of the surgeries.

Fellow patients, having suffered full-on heart attacks, could tell much more terrifying tales of their time under the knife.

One told us that when she awoke from the heavy anesthesia, she looked with astonishment at the reacovery room wall and, in her first moment of consciousness and relief, could see right through the plaster to the world beyond. It's that kind of experience.

I, on the other hand, had gone through a "minimally invasive procedure."

In July, I had become one of the legions of men and women in greater New Haven and far-flung places who have trusted the YNHH team with this 21st century advancement, referred to by the acronym, TAVR (transcatheter aortic valve replacement).

In my case, surgeons drove the new valve, with cells from a cow, through my groin and up an artery all the way to my faulty aortic mechanism. In short, a life-saving adventure.

Now, I am finishing the second half of that adventure. And it had been both a difficult and enlightening one. Difficult because the bar and stakes were high.

The group that supervised us included a physical therapist, Skyler Ocetnik, who was part of a local team of athletes that won this fall's Mid-Atlantic CrossFit Championship in Baltimore, and would go on to compete in national competitions.

I feared he might have little sympathy for a fellow of modest physical capacities, as I had checked my resume and found no listing of CrossFit triumphs. Of course, it's true that three decades ago I ran the 10-mile Guilford road race and was quite pleased with myself until, in the final stretch, a group of walkers passed me.

I know at this point you're wondering what makes the Yale Rehabilitation/Occupational building different from a typical gym?

Well, for one, there is close attention from an expert team of registered nurses — including Jana, Sierra and Jenn — who measure each patient's vital signs during the sessions.

The nutritionist, Nowen, asks patients to make lists of everything (even the secret 10 p.m. Cheetos) they eat over several days, and is gentle in her admonishments. She wouldn't think of blurting out, "You blithering idiot. If you don't stop gorging on saturated fat, sugar and sodium this very day, you'll fall into a coma a week from next Tuesday."

Instead, she makes quiet suggestions for a more balanced and yet satisfying way to consider what we put in our mouths, dishing out recipes that seem influenced by the Mediterranean diet. (Although missing the broiled turkey testicles I once tried in Jerusalem. How could I not? It would have been like passing on the pickle soup in New Britain's "Little Poland.")

As for Skyler and the team of nurses, they jack up the physical challenge over time, and constantly express the idea that "you can do it." And you can do these aerobic machines and resistance training (mostly weights) while the sound system plays, by request from the patients, the Beatles, Carole King, the Stones, Dylan, Johnny Cash, and the Grateful Dead. We peddled to the beat, grateful that we were not yet dead.

On that Friday, I was the only one set to "graduate" from the program, requiring 36 sessions. The others were still in their initial weeks.

It just so happened, too, that this was the final day for Skyler, too. This CrossFit champ had accepted a position in private industry, and would begin the following Monday, without so much as a day off between gigs. He's that kind of guy.

In our final moments together, I told him of my own plan. I said, "I just rejoined the gym I belonged to before the pandemic, mActivity in East Rock. But, Skyler, tell me, is it enough to just join, or do I actually have to go there?"

He thought about it for a minute, consulted with the nurses, and reported that it is the general consensus of the group that going to gym would be more helpful to the soul and the flesh than plunking down on the sofa and watching dismal cable news.

Every session, we received handout sheets of bullet points about heart health, including recipes and an anatomy chart. These pages didn't read much like bodice-ripping novels, but are useful.

One of them was on stress reduction. Seizing on this one day as I was going nowhere fast on the treadmill, Jana and I had the idea the training could be expanded to feature the message, "Don't Take the Bait," counsel on how to keep your ticker working while putting up with relatives whose political opinions nauseate you.

Maybe that's not possible. Though the advice given at the

rehab center is wise, there are limits to practical solutions in our often heartbreaking society.

Yet to end on a positive note. Though the old brownstone hosts a gym you don't really want to belong to, it's so valuable when and if you need it.

As I collected my stuff for the last time, the team gave me my final score — I was exiting the programs nearly ten pounds lighter, but had gained power (my hand gripping strength had increased by nearly 50 percent), my body mass index measure improved, and my blood pressure levels finally fell into the normal range. The team also gave me a thank-you note. Me!

Leaving left a bittersweet feeling, as I headed to the elevator and my renewed life.

Oh, Deer: Creatures of Darkest New Haven

Members of our early morning klatch at the East Rock coffee shop alerted me to the news. A frightened animal had apparently mistaken the bustle of Orange Street for the expanses of East Rock Park and tried to sprint away from creatures she naturally considered cruel and unusual: human beings.

One of the witnesses pointed out there was a certain measure of shock and awe in the neighborhood.

Nutmeggers are generally aware that the state is overrun with these hoofed mammals, nearly 100,000, though the number is an estimate, as the deer haven't yet submitted their census forms. Yet, it is presumed that coffee shops and Italian markets are not common destinations.

This is true although some years ago a buck that had just been grazed by a car wandered in his stupor into a Madison bait and tackle shop. The owner later told me that he circled the aisles a few times, dripped blood on the floor, exacerbated his wounds by ramming against the glass on the back door trying to escape, but never disturbed the merchandise before retreating to the front door, which the owner had opened, and out to the relative safety of the nearby meadow where he licked his wounds. I suggested that the proprietor put up a sign with a slightly altered version of a Harry Truman doctrine: "The Buck Shops Here."

The recent Orange Street deer incident wasn't the only East Rock sighting of late. A doe, in some measure of distress, jumped off of the Mill River bridge into the water below. She seemed to sense that the river is deeper on the east side of the bridge, which made for a safer dive.

And then there was the specimen discovered in another unlikely spot: the administration office of Quinnipiac University, in Hamden. It was there that in the summer of 2019 I took my college-shopping granddaughter for a campus tour, and we watched as a doe approached us at lightning speed, as if worried it might be too late to apply for the next freshman class.

These encounters triggered a recall of other meetings with these agile but not altogether brilliant animals.

One morning in 2015, just after we had moved into our house, I looked out of the back window and saw a doe. She was on her knees, seemed almost asleep, so didn't notice me at first. And when she finally did, she performed that magic that only certain animals master—jumping over the fences that separate backyards on her way back to the park greenery.

The idea of a deer, here in the city, startled me. I thought, as we were new then to New Haven, it must be some sort of omen. The natural world saying, "Hey, you lived in the woods for three decades and now you've abandoned us, but we forgive you because, understandably, at your advancing age, you want to live closer to the theater and concerts and lectures, which we don't have a lot of in the wilds."

Back in Chester, a family of deer (between seven and nine) was almost always present on the hill below the house.

There was a connection between the deer, which continually found our garden the source of easy cuisine, and myself.

When one of the members of the group turned up lame, I saw the limits in her movement, and thought I came to her rescue, putting out a bucket of water every morning. This only meant that she drank from it after eating the parsley, sage, rosemary and, yes, Paul Simon, thyme.

Over one summer she and I developed a kind of relationship. I told her—she was a captive audience because of her delicate condition, and I love captive audiences—that I had once in my life been an expert on deer.

This, as it turned out, was something of an exaggeration. In the summer of 1963, well before Chester or New Haven appeared on the horizon, I became a tour guide in the Upper Peninsula of Michigan. The U.P. to those in the know.

Back then, before anyone ever heard of the term "climate change," a deer was something you saw first in a children's book, then in a Disney film.

If you wanted to see a real Bambi in civilized portions of the Midwest, you had to drive up through Detroit, Lansing, Petoskey, and Mackinac Island to the little town of Hulbert.

And there, on the riverboat on the way to the falls of the Tahquamenon River, I would regale you with the lore of deer in the surrounding forest and point out with delight anytime we'd spot one on the shore slurping the tea-colored water.

That summer, I wore a flannel shirt and an agate tie, looking very much like a nature expert, though some of the time I was making things up, or otherwise disguising my general ignorance of natural wonders.

Twenty years later, of course, Bambi turned into Cruella De Ville. Some new and complex illness was being reported on the Connecticut shoreline, and it appeared as if she was the savage source of it.

Nowadays, Lyme Disease still baffles medical experts and their patients, and we no longer think of deer as mere innocents.

Just before the Lyme discovery, however, New Haven's own Richard Selzer, the late surgeon and author, had warned readers against basing their assessments of such beloved creatures on thin evidence. He wrote an essay in the magazine I edited in which he made the point that humans are suckers. He asked, why on earth do we favor the deer and despise the tiger?

In large part, of course, it's the Aw Factor, as in, "Aw, isn't she cute," which isn't the nature of other beasts. It doesn't help, also, that tigers are omnivores, even interested in consuming latte lovers, should they have the opportunity.

As a survivor of Chester's wilderness, where no lions roam

but where fisher cats, red foxes and coyotes are in residence, I saw Selzer's point but only to a point.

To be sure, our lives in the city have been enriched by less-frightening species. For some reason, a mother robin built a nest on the railing of our back porch a few years ago and protected the blue eggs until three young'uns emerged and learned to fly.

Adult robins now find our backyard irresistible so, of course. we believe these are the former hatchlings coming home.

For years, our bluebird house has been empty, but this spring small avians built a nest inside. Suzanne thinks they're house wrens but since they weren't bluebirds she wasn't too interested. We'll have a fuller report once we witness some floundering first flights.

Today, as I write this, is Father's Day and we remember our lost dads, even reminding each other that we're orphans. A found dead robin in the garden this morning unsettled us but Suzanne took it as a *memento mori*. We try to make the best of things, try to figure out whys and wherefores and deer ones, while ordering our early morning coffees.

The Art of Pill Chasing: A User's Guide

5:45 a.m. You drive from your house with two passengers aboard: your wife and the puppy. The puppy is along for the ride because he never wants to be left behind, even for a trip to the St. Raphael campus of Yale New Haven Hospital.

6:07 a.m. You arrive seven minutes late because the traffic light at the corner of Whalley and Sherman avenues refuses to turn green. "Crap," you say, or actually a cruder four-letter facsimile. Still, at that point you have no idea just how much the fates will turn against you today. You run the red light. Even so, you are more than seven minutes late because the instructions are to drop off the patient at the hospital and you foolishly think this means the entrance. The fine print, however, says she needs to come in through the garage. As you learn later, the staff sends a golf cart to fetch her.

6:15 a.m. On the way home, you recall your own similar foot surgery, performed three years earlier on your arthritic and aching big toe, and that in the aftermath you forgot to take your pain pills and spent a night in agony. "This won't happen to her," you mutter. "I'll be sure of it."

8:12 a.m. You and the puppy are home, as you catch up on the morning's dreadful news out of Washington, D.C. Your iPhone pings with an automated message. Your wife's procedure is finished. You tell this news to the puppy, who at the moment is chewing off yet another eraser from one of your mechanical pencils.

9:10 a.m. You have a remote Pilates session scheduled with your instructor in two hours and wonder if that will be possible, given that this morning, you realize, is not all about you. A nurse calls to report your wife is ready for pickup but before you arrive you must go to the drugstore for her prescription – pain pills. Yes, of course, you say, wanting to avoid the fate you suffered. You load the puppy in the crate in the back of the car, and say, "We're going off to the Walgreens in Hamden." This is because, of course, the little pharmacy just a brief walk from your front door shut its door a few years ago.

9:20 a.m. The window of the pharmacy, which is supposed to be open at 9 a.m., is closed. How can that be? I inquire. The store, it turns out, is short of pharmacists and that heaven only knows when one will arrive. You've been hearing a lot about shortages lately, including computer chips for automobiles, prompting you to hope that your 2008 Saab will hold out until the chip market rebounds, or at least until you can get a pain pill to your wife.

9:40 a.m. You arrive at what you think is the pickup place for patients, in the George Street Garage. You are mistaken, however, because the garage lacks clear signage. So you don't see your wife in her wheelchair, and try to call her but because you are in a concrete jungle the call fails. "Crap," you say, only the word you use, again, is not that one. Finally, you find the right garage level, and your wife seems pleased to have the whole thing over, but you know the whole thing isn't over because the pain pills are still nonexistent.

9:45 a.m. As you reach the corner of Elm and Church, you see the editor of the New Haven Independent riding his bicycle to his office. But you don't get a chance to shout, "Hey, Paul, it's me," and then, "I won't have an essay for you about today's troubles because they're not yet annoying enough to write about." In this, your prediction is as accurate as the night in November 2016 you assured your wife that Donald J. Trump would never become president.

9:50 a.m. Your wife dials the pharmacy from the passenger seat. A recorded voice says, in effect, "Thank you for calling even if you are in dire need of pain pills but there are 493 callers ahead of you and they're not talking to anybody because nobody is there. Have a great day."

9:57 a.m. You prop your wife on the couch, and ask, "Are you having any pain?" She is not. Yet. So you have a window, even if it's a small one. You and the pup head again to the pharmacy because by now someone with a degree in pharmacology certainly must have arrived. But no. You ask the woman who appears to be the manager to transfer the prescription to the other Walgreens in Hamden. "Can't do it," she says. "It's a controlled substance. Those aren't transferable. The doctor must re-prescribe it." You argue, to no avail, and think of the scene in the film "Casablanca," and Bogie's line that three little people don't amount to a hill of beans in this crazy world. In this case, two little people and their dog.

9:58 a.m. You call your wife about the need for a new script. She dials her doctor's office as you and the pup go to Hamden's other Walgreens. But the queue at the pharmacy looks like one of those bread lines from the Great Depression, with the other Walgreens service closed. "Crap," you opine again.

10:17 a.m. The nice if frazzled pharmacy technician at the counter tells you that no order for a controlled substance has arrived, and that you should return in an hour. You call your wife, who calls her doctor's office again, and is told that the surgeon is busy cutting up a patient.

11:02 a.m. You return home with no pain pills, instead some nice butternut squash soup for her from Atticus Market.

1:10 p.m. Your wife gets a call from the surgeon's office. A script has been written and sent to the Walgreens that actually has a pharmacy open. You rush out there with the pup, figuring the painkiller the hospital dispensed will wear off soon.

1:37 p.m. But now that pharmacy window is closed. "Lunch break," an employee says. This is a new thing. It used to be that a person could go to a pharmacy at any time but now if you arrive between 1:30 and 2 p.m., you must go back out to the car, let the pup out, and take him to the bench overlooking Whitney Avenue. There, he spots a discarded paper coffee cup, starts to lap up the grande latte, or whatever it is, even as you remind him that caffeine, like avocados, grapes and raisins, is toxic for canines.

2 p.m. You go back inside. But you've miscalculated, as once again a bread line has formed, mostly of women older than you. You can't very well say, "Excuse me, all, but I've been waiting all day for urgent medication for my wife so will all you please step aside." So you stick with the facsimile of "crap." However, the nice technician calls you over and says, "Don't worry, it'll only be 15 minutes." By now the tech and I are on a first name basis.

2:37 p.m. It's ready. But as she rings you up, a pharmacist appears and says, "This is a form of morphine and it seems your wife is allergic to morphine. You say you'll check, so you call her and ask and she says something like, "Whaaa?" You pass the test. The pills are yours.

2:57 p.m. You arrive home. You let the pup out of the car and head for the house. Halfway there you realize you left the prescription in the Saab. Hah. Well, what a nice surprise ending to a tale, which certainly now is one you can submit to Paul at the Independent. But you are wrong about the ending.

2:58 p.m. Your wife is in bed, her left foot propped up. You say, "I've brought you the pain pills at last." She says, "Thanks. I'm fine. I don't think I need them."

A Miracle, Deconstructed

The long road from New Haven to the old industrial city of Erie, Pa., passes through Danbury, Binghamton, Damascus, Homs, Tripoli, Beirut, Chicago, and finally to the shore of the Great Lake that Erie is named after.

At least that's the route we took in our minds when we undertook the ten-hour drive to, at last, meet the whole family of Haitham Dalati and Shiyam Daghestani, for whom, under the auspices of IRIS, we had helped ease their transition from the Syrian civil war to life in New Haven. This was before they moved in 2019 to a more economical city where a community of similar refugees had sprouted.

After nearly four long years of the family's separation as a result of Trump's Muslim travel ban (though it was not officially called that in order, in large part, to get it through the Supreme Court), we'd already celebrated one miracle.

The news from Erie that on Thanksgiving, 2020, despite overwhelming odds, their dearest wish had come true. They were together again, sobbing joyfully in each other's arms.

How, precisely, this happened is still not clear to us, as Trump was still in office. I knew only that Suzanne and I had asked every person in public office we knew, and many we didn't, for help.

If, collectively, we couldn't significantly address the Jewish aspiration of *tikkun olam*, the repair of the world, a tall order, we could at least repair the world of one family at a time.

Even so, we had not yet met the six new refugees. We couldn't let the story end without seeing for ourselves how these intrepid immigrants fit into their new place.

The family roster: Farah, who is Haitham and Shiyam's daughter, her husband, Wesam, a baker, their four children, Layla, then 17, Haitham, 16, Lamese, 13, and Aboudi, 8. How were they adjusting to America, their Promised Land back in their darkest hours?

We had worried about the change of culture for all. The six members of the family left behind in exile in Lebanon had faced hard times there.

The country had been overwhelmed by corruption, violence, a fierce environmental explosion, bigotry against refugees from Syria in large part due to religious differences but also the collapse of the Lebanese economy that kept Farah and the others frightened, not only for their safety but ability to provide for their basic needs.

We were concerned that for the children, in particular, the legacy of all that would negatively affect their psyche and prospects in America. We remembered of course the intensity and courage that little Aboudi showed when he wanted to speak directly to Donald Trump to convince him that his family was not a terrorist group.

The ride, obviously, was long and taxing for drivers of our stage of life. Three hours is usually my limit. But we thought of what our Syrian friends had gone through—including having their two houses destroyed, escaping through the woods and across borders, finding sanctuary in Tripoli, then the terrible separation caused by a perverse figure in the White House—and we dismissed any ache or pain or impatience to get to the old manufacturing city.

When the drive ended, Haitham and Shiyam were waiting for us, and we all shed some tears over that. She had some Syrian pastry ready, something Haitham had to wait in line to get and only available on certain days. "We are so glad to see you," Haitham said. "Good, good," Shiyam said, wiping her eyes.

They looked very much the same to us, though there was more color in Shiyam's face, and the emotion expressed was of a different measure, a prodigious sense of relief. So often we had entered their home knowing that sadness would come to the fore. Not this time.

They showed us the rooms of their tidy two-story apartment, probably the same amount of space as their former home back in Westville but somehow seeming smaller. "Enough for us," Haitham said. "We are happy here."

Haitham told us that their daughter, Farah, and her husband, Wesam, and their four children—all of whom we had only seen in photographs—had moved less than a quarter mile away in the same complex.

This was Haitham's doing; for all of the hardships, he has found his footing in Erie as a man who still can get things done. So he found a spacious corner apartment, had it repainted and otherwise refurbished.

When we made the short drive through the complex to Farah's apartment, our headlights shone on her building. The backdoor opened and, as Farah welcomed us, she wrapped her arms around Suzanne and the two of them had a moment.

The rest of the family, with the exception of young Haitham, named after his grandfather, who was off playing the high school soccer team, was lined up in the kitchen to greet us. The oldest daughter, Layla, in perfect English and with great ease and comfort, said, "It is so wonderful to meet you. Thank you so much for everything."

Wesam stood quietly by, smiling but not talking, appearing to be unsure about his language skills in America. The other children spoke fine English to us, though little Aboudi, at eight years old, seemed more reticent than the little boy who wanted the White House phone number. But he also was shy, and didn't want us to see that he wasn't as fluent in the new language as his siblings.

We could see right away what a beautiful apartment it

was, with an old-world feel, refinished wooden floors, some of them covered by lovely area rugs.

After our tour of their house all we sat in the spacious living room, a feast of candies, cookies and fruits placed before us on the coffee table. The children were all attentive, not one staring at a screen.

Suzanne and I felt it was important to ask how they were finding their places in America, and anything else they wanted to tell us. Layla was the first to speak up. She was preparing to choose a college to attend.

"What will you study?" I asked.

"I hope, after undergraduate studies, to go to medical school."

"Will you pursue a specialty?"

"Pathology," she said. And I thought at least three things simultaneously.

How was it that a child like her, charming and bright and having by then studied less than a year in American schools, put herself in a position to reach so high?

What was her experience here, considering that she arrived here from two shattered countries in the Middle East?

And, more pointedly and perhaps unfairly, why would a person with such an open and engaging personality want to sit over a microscope all day and not have interaction with patients?

On that last point, she was clear. "I believe I will meet a lot of patients in my work, and help them."

The answers to the other points astonished me. The children, with the exception of Aboudi, felt confident in school, and were considered to be among the top students.

"I'm thrilled to hear it," I said. "But how is that in your second language, and having grown up in very troubled societies, that you can learn so much in such a short time?"

Layla took up the prompt. "The things we're studying

here, in Erie schools, are things we learned three years ago in Lebanon."

It is foolish, of course, to use anecdotal evidence from one family and make sweeping conclusions. Still, I'm tempted to ask how is it that a country that doesn't really exist in terms of order, justice and competence—in a great sense in a battle with itself—seems to surpass by leaps and bounds America's educational system? Should I really be surprised?

We have read lately that the United States does not rank as high in the world as we presumed in terms of education, and comparative test scores in math and science. And while all such statistics are suspect, haven't so many of us found it hard to believe that Americans can be so gullible, so ignorant about basic information.

Moreover, such ignorance of late has been celebrated and rewarded. Finally, a government for lazy minds. Finally, freedom to be oblivious to fact and still be a part of a political power base.

In Erie the next night, the night after young Haitham had scored two goals for the Erie High soccer team, we learned of his erudition, his mastery of English, and in similar fashion of his sister, Layla, his refined manners.

But the moment that stuck with us most then and afterwards was when Farah, who is less confident in her English than her children, took out her cellphone and called up something she had written in our language, not trusting herself to be able to remember what to say in the moment, considering the emotion of it.

She read, "We would all like to thank you, Suzanne and Lary, for what you did for us to help us come to this country, and to take care of my parents."

I didn't get to the end of her sentence before I felt tears coming down on my cheeks. I didn't think of it at the time, but on the drive home, I understood that the horror of the story of the family, the help it needed, the playing out of the story, the final moments of joy, were all a part of what city life like that in New Haven demands of us.

We are not meant to hide away in a barn house in the woods, as I had, for all of our days. We are meant to try to do what we can to help each other, to repair the world, to support the locals like IRIS who help, to likely fail at this effort, but, on the rarest of occasions, to be able to shout, "Hallelujah!"

The Dog Ate My Implant

It took me more than seven decades to get into Yale, not as an undergrad but as a lecturer. It took our pooch, Lucca, only fifteen months to receive his notice of acceptance as a student.

In late February, 2022, he passed his entrance exam at the university's Canine Cognition Center on St. Ronan Street. The general intent of the place, according to the website, is to discover "how dogs think about the world." Lucca's world, by comparison to ours, seems unburdened by painful news and worries.

So, when asked to find hidden treats in a three-card monte trick and pay attention to a video—feats equivalent, apparently, to a high school human who boasts a 4.0 GPA and captains the debate team—he focused only on those tests.

As a result, he now owns a sheepskin, or facsimile, that verifies our Lagotto Romagnolo is a "dog scholar." It is signed by none other than Dr. Laurie Santos, who has presided over the most popular course ever at Bulldog U., on the keys to happiness.

It's a good thing, however, that she and her colleagues do not test the intelligence and competence of dog owners. If these were ever recorded and reviewed by the school's behavioral scientists, I'd end up on probation.

It wouldn't help me to point out I've never had a dog before, and therefore am a sucker for Lucca's affection. The fact is I'm not a reliable purveyor of the discipline required of anyone who owns such a pet. Whenever I say "No," to him, only sixteen times a typical day, he tilts his head, as if to say, "Really?" And too often, I back off.

When I walk in the door after spending hours on campus, he seems happy to see me, but in a second has absconded with my scarf or gloves.

At such a point, I don't sit him down and say, "If you do

that again, I won't take you to Disneyworld."

Could I put a value on the inventory that Lucca has ruined? Yes. Shoes alone: maybe $500.

But what price is that to pay for a guy who every morning climbs up on the bed to lick my left eyelid? (Why he never licks my right eyelid is an issue I intend to take up with his therapist.)

On the other hand, there is his latest caper to consider.

As an English Department faculty member, I gird myself for some version of, "The dog ate my homework." Indeed, Yale students are clever, too clever to offer that explanation.

But how to excuse my recent incident at home, something that on the retail market may have cost me at least $2,500 if the timing had been different?

At my age, I am among the legions of seniors who need a little help eating and smiling. That is, I used to tell people that the reason I didn't go to dental school was that as a youngster I couldn't count to 32, the preferred number of choppers.

The joke, however, was on me. I never would have to count that high, given the number of original teeth I would end up with.

Yale may one day offer a course, Math 320: Lary Bloom's Big Mouth: Subtract 22 From 32, add 16 for Implants That Didn't Take, 9 That Did, Divide by 16 in a Plastic Plate, and What Do You Get? This is one to stump even Lucca.

This Ivy Leaguer isn't intuitive enough to distinguish a piece of kibble from a titanium dental implant that, having seen its better days, escaped from the receding bone in the upper jaw.

How the incident happened: I, of course, had done what any human would do when I noticed something was missing in my mouth. I picked it up off the floor, issued the required "Oh, what kind of fool am I?" but, providing further proof of the charge, placed the well-used metal screw on the counter in the bathroom.

I knew very well that Lucca seldom leaves potential food

unnoticed, but thought, hey, this probably isn't very appetizing. Then, as Suzanne and I were on a Zoom call with friends, an alarm went off in my head—what if...

It was too late. I got to the bathroom just as Lucca inhaled the implant, made with an element that possibly came from, of all places, Ukraine, a major exporter of titanium. My attempts to get him to throw it up went for naught. I called my periodontist, who of course has heard many stories over his years in practice. But never this one.

At first, he worried this was the new implant that he'd screwed into my head just weeks earlier. "No," I explained, "this is one from the old days." Relieved, he seconded my view that it was no longer of use, though seemed skeptical that it might fetch a few dollars on eBay.

He changed the subject to Lucca's welfare. Indeed, it is well known that dogs can get severe reactions to chocolate or raisins or onions, though I haven't come across any expert who yet has added dental implants to that list.

I was reminded of a Facebook post by another Lagotto owner who said her pooch ate her grandmother's diamond earrings, and so a poop-snoop posse had to be organized, which eventually discovered the missing ice in a pile.

Our story has a similarly happy ending. As it turned out, there was no need for panic. It all, apparently, came out in the end. Somewhere.

From Bruno Mars to the Geezer Top 40

I saw her first when our party of four walked into the mezzanine at the Shubert Theater. She stood out among the ushers as by far the youngest, perhaps a high school student. All the others had accumulated much more life experience, enough of it to turn their hair gray, a fact that fit them nicely into the evening's crowd.

The young usher would have preferred to work a concert by her idol, Bruno Mars, who might perform "That's What I Like" or "Grenade" or "Locked Out of Heaven."

Alas, she was knocked out of that heavenly thought on a mid-October night, stuck helping patrons arrive for a string of musical pearls by a group called the Glenn Miller Orchestra. What on earth was that? And why were so many geezers like me coming through these mezzanine doors?

Actually, it wasn't so many; the mezzanine was but half full, not the standing-room-only crowd that in the Shubert's golden days came to see one of more than 600 tryouts of shows headed to Broadway, or even these days, when it is often packed for popular musicals that, after success in Manhattan, have sent out road shows.

From her perch in the back of the section, the young usher could see all the aging heads, none of them with vibrant shocks of hair like hers, or, I dare say, more than a handful of representatives from the city's minority communities.

And when the curtain opened, and she saw the band of seventeen members and a conductor, the picture was clearly un-representative of her life in New Haven. The stage was filled with men, almost all of them white; a fair representation of what once was, but a statement in itself. Nostalgia makes no accommodation for diversity.

During the first of two sets, she might have glanced down

in our row, where she would have seen my own gray head bobbing up and down and around to the beat of relics like "Pennsylvania 6-5000," inspired by a call Glenn Miller made from a place referred to in those days as a phone booth. She might have wondered why I swooned as the band members stood to play Miller's composition and signature tune, "Moonlight Serenade," featuring his unique reed sound produced by four saxophones and one clarinet—a sound that for a brief moment in time—1938 to 1942, a period when the world turned dark— sent America dancing and dreaming.

The young usher in the back would have seen me standing when the conductor and host for the evening, the slick Nick Hilscher, asked all service veterans to rise, and then dedicated "American Patrol" to us.

The usher, I figured, must know of veterans of more recent wars. She was just a few years older than I was in 1954 when my parents took me to see the film, "The Glenn Miller Story," with Jimmy Stewart and June Allyson. That night at the movies opened my eyes and ears. I loved that music.

"In the Mood," I was transported to "Tuxedo Junction" and, along the way, drinking from a "Little Brown Jug." How could I explain such a revelation to a teenage usher? Probably no way. On the other hand, I wouldn't hold it against her. I am not Paul Lynde, singing in "Bye, Bye Birdie," that lament ("Kids, I don't know what's wrong with these kids today"). They're entitled to their music, and to what moves them, and who's to say it's not as artistic or more so than what drew me in at that age. Still … .

At intermission, I noticed the teenage usher again. I asked her if she'd ever heard this music before. She was polite. "I think a little of it in school." But it was mostly new to her. That's when I asked her how old she was (sixteen), who her favorite musician was (Mars), which relieved me a bit because I didn't have to say, "Who's that?" I knew the name, if not the work. I asked, "Are there any songs that Bruno Mars sings that I would like?"

She looked me over for a moment and said, "I don't think so." I said, smiling, "You really know how to hurt an old guy."

She laughed. I liked her spunk, the ease and politeness with which she spoke to someone five times her age.

By the second half of the program, audience members were all lost in time, almost literally blown away by heavy brass — four trombonists and four trumpeters. The "girl singer," Hannah Truckenbrod, and the new version of the vocalist group, The Modernaires, offered "Blues in the Night."

I recalled the old Miller film, and that the bandleader disbanded his group in 1942 to form a new military band to entertain the troops overseas, and that, alas, the small plane he took from England to France disappeared in the mist over the English Channel. But, unlike other such tragic endings, this one had an afterlife.

The Glenn Miller Orchestra has been touring the world since 1956, and it was our turn. For the next night, the band was to perform at New York City's Town Hall before embarking on its fall tour to dozens of destinations.

To that end, we all, at least metaphorically, came aboard the "Chattanooga Choo Choo," which, by the way, no longer runs along the tracks even if the tune, number one on the charts in 1941, still does. And by the time the encore came, "Farewell Blues," I had been through the emotional wringer. But I kept my composure as, walking out, I saw the teenage usher for the third time.

I asked her, "What did you think of the music?"

She said, "Amazing."

I said, "Really?"

She said, "Yes."

And as I left the mezzanine, there was a hop in my geezer step.

Lary Bloom, who moved from Chester, CT to New Haven in 2015, is a prolific writer. His books, some of them co-authored, include *Sol LeWitt: A Life of Ideas*; *The Writer Within*; *Letters From Nuremberg*; *The Ignorant Maestro*; *The Test of Our Times*; and *Lary Bloom's Connecticut Notebook*. His plays include *Worth Avenue*, *Wild Black Yonder*, and the musical *A Woman of a Certain Age*, for which he was the lyricist. He has taught writing at Yale, Wesleyan, Trinity College, and in Fairfield University's MFA in Creative Writing program. His columns and essays have appeared in the *New York Times*, the *Miami Herald*, the *Hartford Courant*, *Connecticut Magazine* and the *New Haven Independent*. He can be reached at larybloom@gmail.com.

This book is set in Garamond Premier Pro, which had its genesis in 1988 when type-designer Robert Slimbach visited the Plantin-Moretus Museum in Antwerp, Belgium, to study its collection of Claude Garamond's metal punches and typefaces. During the fifteen hundreds, Garamond — a Parisian punch-cutter — produced a refined array of book types that combined an unprecedented degree of balance and elegance, for centuries standing as the pinnacle of beauty and practicality in type-founding. Slimbach has created a new interpretation based on Garamond's designs and on compatible italics cut by Robert Granjon, Garamond's contemporary.

Copies of this book can be ordered
at any bookstore
or directly from the author:
Lary Bloom
850 Orange St.
New Haven, CT 06511.
Send $18 per book
plus $4 shipping
by check payable
to Lary Bloom.

•

For more information on the work of Lary Bloom
visit www.antrimhousebooks.com/authors.html.
You can reach the author at
Larybloom@gmail.com.

www.ingramcontent.com/pod-product-compliance
Lightning Source LLC
Chambersburg PA
CBHW021222130726
47988CB00002B/778